T0115180

What readers are saying about *Hog Washed*...

"What a wonderful book! The imagery is funny, heartwarming, wistful and simply beautiful. As a member of Deeper Life Fellowship I have always enjoyed Dr. Wyatt's teaching. He has so much wisdom and insight into the heart of God and simply has a beautiful talent for sharing that insight. I knew it was going to be good, but did not expect this. Well done Mark!"

—Bill Starling

"Hog Washed is another example of Mark Wyatt's unique perspective and insight. It helps brings fresh revelation to timeless Biblical truths!"

—Greg Pollard

"There are times when you can't see a star when you look straight at it—the beauty of its light only registers when you are focused on something else. As you read this incredible little book, you will find yourself so completely caught up in the story of Reggie that you may not notice, until after you have closed the back cover, that the truth of your own belonging has snuck in from the side."

—Brad Sutton, *pastor*
Point Church
Little Elm, TX

"Dr. Mark Wyatt joins C.S. Lewis and John Bunyan in the genre of Christian allegory. *Hog Washed* is a fun fictional story about a pig and a dog that reveals a profound truth. I found it to be enjoyable, educational and inspirational."

—David Brumbaugh

"This is a great story about the longing for a greater love."

—Matthew Helms

"Pastor Mark facilitates the passion of the Father's heart to yours as you drink in His love and goodness. This book is worth reading because it leads you into a relationship with God that is so profound that you can live there permanently. Read with your heart open and receive an upgrade in your thinking that will change your life."

—Andrea Hartman

"*Hog Washed* is a wonderful story about Reggie, a little pig that wants a better life, and how it relates to our wanting a better life, too. I could not put the story down! I finished it in one day and plan to reread it for all the nuances that I might have missed the first time. This story makes the concept of *sonship* so understandable. It's not about what we do, but what has been done for us."

—Debi Collette

Also by Dr. Mark Wyatt:

The New Normal: Experiencing the Unstoppable Move of God (2011)

HOG WASHED

A SMALL FABLE ABOUT A BIG CHANGE

BY

MARK WYATT

WESTBOW
PRESS
A DIVISION OF THOMAS NELSON

WestBow Press books may be ordered through booksellers or by contacting:

WestBow Press
A Division of Thomas Nelson
1663 Liberty Drive
Bloomington, IN 47403
www.westbowpress.com
1-(866) 928-1240

Because of the dynamic nature of the Internet, any web addresses or
links contained in this book may have changed since publication and
may no longer be valid. The views expressed in this work are solely those
of the author and do not necessarily reflect the views of the publisher,
and the publisher hereby disclaims any responsibility for them.

Any people depicted in stock imagery provided by Thinkstock are models,
and such images are being used for illustrative purposes only.

Certain stock imagery © Thinkstock.

ISBN: 978-1-4497-6184-4 (sc)
ISBN: 978-1-4497-6185-1 (e)

Library of Congress Control Number: 2012913968

Printed in the United States of America

WestBow Press rev. date: 08/02/2012

Contents

Acknowledgements

It is said that writing a book is long, lonely work and that every author knows the primal terror of staring at a blank page, fingers hovering over the keyboard, waiting for genius to strike. While that may be true, it is also true that no author holds the finished book in his hands without a lot of other hands helping along the way. The book you now hold in your hands is no exception, and so, a hearty "thank you" is in order for a number of people:

- To Dudley Hall, whose teaching on the subject of orphans and sons opened the floodgates of freedom for me in that upstairs room in Waxahachie, Texas.

Because of that moment, I will always be able to point to the exact square inch of carpet where I heard the Father call me "son" in a way I had never heard before.

- To Jack Taylor, whose investment in me has revealed God's Father-heart these past years, as he made himself available to me like I was the only one he loved. Thank you, Papa Jack.

- To the brothers of the Fellowship of Connected Churches and Ministries and the Kerygma Network, for being as arrested by this revelation as I was, and for helping me discover the boundless depths of the brotherhood of sons.

- To all the Kickstarter backers who helped make this book a reality, especially my Dad, Gene Wyatt, Sr., Melvin and Libby Badon, Milton and Ann Varner, Bobby and Shirley Varner, Shane and Amy Collette, Doug and Ramona O'Brien, Jason O'Brien, and my brother, Rick Wyatt. Thank you for putting your money where my mouth is!

- To the Staff, the Elders, and the people of Deeper Life Fellowship, for the freedom and the encouragement to put into words the things that have changed us forever. Ain't nobody like the Deep Sheep!

- And, of course, to my wife, Mary Ann, and my children—Samuel, Sarah, Nathaniel, and Autumn—for making my life count.

For Mary Ann

"I never met a pig I didn't like. *All* pigs are intelligent, emotional, and sensitive souls. They *all* love company. They *all* crave contact and comfort. Pigs have a delightful sense of mischief; most of them seem to enjoy a good joke and appreciate music. And that is something you would certainly never suspect from your relationship with a pork chop."

— Sy Montgomery
The Good Good Pig: The Extraordinary Life of Christopher Hogwood

"How happy are those who reside in Your house, who praise You continually."

—*Psalm 84:4*

Author's Note

What you are about to read is allegory, an illustration of what I believe to be one of the most transforming, life-changing, freedom-giving truths that God is speaking to the Body of Christ today. It is the story of a pig who longs to be somewhere he has never seen, but knows that when he is there, he will find the life that he knows is possible. The message contained in this little story is being echoed around the globe, it is a sound coming from many different streams and from every corner of Christianity. It is the sound of sonship.

As I was writing this book, I became aware of some aspects of the story that might make readers remember George Orwell's classic allegory, *Animal*

Farm. While this work is in no way a re-telling of that novel, it is to our advantage to make a few remarks at the outset regarding comparisons and contrasts with it.

In 1945, when George Orwell first published *Animal Farm* in England, it was a scathing condemnation of Communism and the human rights violations of Soviet Russia. In the story, the pigs set themselves up as rulers of the working class while trying to maintain the facade that they are just like the common animals, except smarter and naturally more able to lead this new revolution of freedom from oppression. The problem is that they become corrupted by the power and gradually become more and more like the men they detested at the beginning. The moral of the story? Absolute power corrupts absolutely. *Animal Farm*, however, is born from the earthly reality of a fallen kingdom ruled by fallen men. It portrays the social inevitabilities of self-promotion, envy, and fear.

But what if there was another farm? What if there was a farm where the farmer was good and where the desire for *more* came not from discontentment or selfish ambition, but from the demonstration of a better life? What if there was a farm where a regular pig could dream of being more than just a regular pig?

What if the sun seemed to rise more quickly over Far Away Hill this time of year…?

PART 1

Chapter 1

Mud To The Bone

The sun seemed to rise more quickly over Far Away Hill this time of year, and by the time Reggie opened one eye, he was already miserably hot. It was only midmorning, but the sun pressed on the roof of the old doghouse, which was now a pighouse, and as Reggie sighed, he let out one big snuffle that blew a little path in the hay right in front of his snout. Even in the humid air, he couldn't bear to leave the shade of the pighouse. "Just five more minutes," he mumbled, barely above the sound of a dream.

"No, Reggie, now!" fussed his mother, who had stuck her massive head in the door for the second time in two minutes. "You are the last one still sleeping, so come on, get yourself upright and get out here and eat!" Reggie smacked his lips, blinked his eyes, wiggled his ears, and then he brought his legs up under his body and pushed up, wobbly at first, then steadying over the next few seconds. He lumbered ahead into the sunlight, blinking and turning away before stepping out of the pighouse. Reggie was not yet a full-grown pig, but he wasn't a piglet anymore either. In fact, he was remarkably unremarkable. His mother had named him Regular because there was not one distinguishing mark on him— no tuft of white hair on his forehead, no cute star-shaped birthmark on his hind quarters, not even a memorable mole hiding somewhere on his smooth pig skin. Nor was Reggie particularly big or small. The farmer had rubbed his ears once and told him that he wasn't quite a "finishing pig," that he wasn't ready for market yet… whatever that meant.

Reggie walked over to the pile of corn, smiled at his mother as he passed by, and took two good-sized cobs into his mouth before turning right and going down the small slope toward the sound of the other young pigs shouting and laughing. As if he were on automatic, Reggie made his way to the ever more familiar mud hole, the wet smell of must and dirt growing stronger in his nostrils as he neared. This, he figured, was the same thing he had done every day, and would do every day, for the rest of his life—

sleeping, waking up, eating corn, and wallowing in the mud hole.

He was almost fully awake now, and ready to find a good spot to chomp his corn, when a squealing little piglet tore past him, laughing, and launched himself into the deepest part of the mud hole- which, actually, only came up to the piglet's knees. The piglet sailed through the air, closed his eyes, squealed even louder, and plopped with a mushy sploosh into the cool, thick mud. The other pigs watching laughed in approval as the next one started down the slope.

Reggie hurried across his path and smiled at the memory of playing the same game himself not long ago. He turned to encourage the clumsy little one barreling toward him. "Straighen up, Jimmy Dean, or you won't get any height!" he yelled. Jimmy Dean was going too fast for himself, and right as he reached the launch site, his feet crossed in front of him and he slid, spinning into the mudhole on his belly, causing wet brown globs to fly through the air and splat onto the spectators, who laughed even harder than before and fell onto their sides in delight. Reggie moved uphole a ways to give them their room, found a spot big enough to surround him, then executed his uniquely Reggian style: he stood, all four feet together, closed his eyes, and fell over, stiff-legged, into the soft, cool mud that he would call his own for the next few hours. Or at least until it was time to eat again.

And there he lay, wet and grimy, one ear twitching away with every tentative landing of two circling flies. He sighed, worked on his corn, and swiveled his head just enough to orient himself in the pen. Reggie's little world of mud lay about three pig lengths from a wooden trough that, as of now, sat empty. He knew, though, that in just a little while, he would hear the whine and grind of the old truck's gears. Then the ground would tremble a little as the board-sided pickup would come bouncing heavily over the rise, with slick, thick, greenish brown waves sloshing over the stained and crusted panels that made the bed into a huge box.

Even as he anticipated its arrival, the truck rose into view, just as he had imagined it. It squealed to a stop on the other side of the fence, and somewhere inside its engine, rods pumped and gears ground again as the farmer forced it into reverse, bringing the old box right over the trough. The farmer shut off the engine, the door squeaked open and the farmer lowered himself out of the cab while he put on his thick leather work gloves. "Soo-wee! Hello piggies!" he said. "Time for your favorite treat!"

The farmer stepped to the back of the truck, removed a pin, threw a latch, grabbed a lever, and pulled. The bottom of the back panel swung out with the force of the liquid inside, and *whoosh, splat, schplunk*, out poured the slop until the trough was overflowing and thick rivers of the liquefied garbage glumped toward the ground.

Instantly, all the playing piglets stopped mid-game and ran over. Reggie knew there was no hurry to get to the trough. Let the little pigs have their fill, there would be plenty left. And there would always be more coming. Reggie had noticed that some of the other animals were fed once a day, and sometimes sparingly. He had heard a word associated with this kind of eating- "diet." He didn't know what it meant, but he didn't want to know. It sounded horrible. Besides, the pigs were always given all that they could eat. Life for Reggie was like another word he had heard the farmer use—what was it? Oh, yeah. A *buffet*.

As Reggie lay in the mud, barely hearing the grunts and splashes of pigs and slop, he began to reflect, which was something pigs were not known to do, normally. But Reggie wasn't like other pigs. Sometimes he would just think. And when he thought, he would wonder. This was one of those times. "I wonder," he thought, "could there be more to being a pig than just mud and slop?" It wasn't that Reggie didn't enjoy mud and slop, but neither did he have some great affection or longing for it. It was just all he had ever known, and it was alright, he guessed. But he dreamed of more.

"'S goin' on, amigo!" Reggie knew that voice immediately, and was smiling before he saw where it was actually coming from.

"Hey, Breezy, what's shakin'?" Reggie greeted the farmer's black-and-white dog as Breezy rounded the front of the truck. Reggie rose from the mud, which was pretty uncomfortable now. The sun had already begun baking it to his body, and when he stood, hard clumps fell off, pulling his hair as they went. "Ouch!" he winced as he sauntered to the fence.

"Beautiful day, ain't it?" said Breezy. People said that dogs don't really smile, but Reggie knew better. Breezy smiled all the time. He came onto the farm out of nowhere, a stray in the truest sense of the word. For the first couple of weeks, the farmer didn't know from one day to the next if the dog would be around. So when he did show up, the farmer started calling him Breezy. When Breezy came around, the farmer fed him, bathed him, petted him, and brought him inside at night. Breezy "came around" more and more, and eventually he figured out where life was good, and one day he just stayed. He had been smiling ever since. Breezy never talked much about his life before the farm, but he sure talked a lot about how good it was now.

"Hey, guess what?" said Breezy.

"I give up," said Reggie.

"But you didn't guess yet."

"Nope. Not gonna, either. What?"

"The farmer's son is coming home!" said the dog.

"He's been gone awhile, hasn't he?" asked Reggie.

"Yeah, the farmer said he has been living in a place called 'College.' Said he's been preparing himself to come home and help his father run the farm. Apparently there's more to all this than what we see. Anyway, he's coming home tomorrow! Isn't that great?"

Reggie shrugged as much as a pig can shrug. "I guess so," he said. "But why is that so great?"

"Why?!" exclaimed Breezy. "Why? I'll tell you why. That's one more person to brush me, feed me, pet me, play with me… a whole other person to love on this lucky dog!"

And as quick as that, a new word floated down onto Reggie's ears. What was that word that Breezy had just used? *Love.* Now that sounded like a great word. Not at all like *diet*.

Chapter 2

The Great Indoors

The next morning, Reggie watched with a new level of interest as Breezy received his weekly grooming from the farmer. He stuck his snout through the pigpen fence and rested his chin on the second rail from the bottom so that he could relax as he watched.

The farmer whistled for Breezy as he held the garden hose over a big washtub, filling it almost to the brim with cold, clear water. Reggie looked down at the mud puddle he was standing in. As Breezy bounded up, barking cheerfully, the farmer rubbed the dog's furry head, smiled and laughed, and when he scratched Breezy behind the ears, Breezy's eyes closed, his smile got wider, and his back right leg twitched in time to the rhythm of the rub. Reggie tried to reach up and rub his own head, but his leg was too short. Then he tried twitching his back leg, but he only lost his balance and staggered a few steps to the left.

Next, the farmer motioned with his hand, and Breezy jumped into the tub. The farmer knelt down, put one hand behind the dog's head, and with his other hand, he scooped up the sparkling water and rubbed it into Breezy's fur until he looked half his normal size. Breezy stood in the water, dripping all over and shivering a little, despite the warm sunshine. The farmer squeezed a green liquid into one hand, then rubbed it into Breezy's coat. This was always Reggie's favorite part to watch. Soon, Breezy was completely white, with only his eyes, nose, and tongue showing through the suds.

The farmer kept rubbing and squeezing, rubbing and squeezing, and Breezy was enjoying every second. After that, the farmer took the bright green water hose and let the water pour all over the dog. This was where Reggie could not help laughing out loud. Breezy the fluffy became Breezy the scrawny. It always amazed Reggie how small and skinny his friend looked at this stage. Finally, the farmer stood, tossed the hose onto the ground, stepped back, and said, "Okay Breezy, fire away!" Breezy then shook like he had been wanting to shake for the last five minutes, and soap flew in every direction, almost as if he had exploded all the love that had just been rubbed into him. Then he jumped out of the washtub like a shot and ran around so fast that all Reggie could see was a black-and-white blur. After a few minutes of watching Breezy roll around in the grass to dry himself, the farmer did something that somehow made Reggie ache with longing- he held open the front door, whistled once, low and soft, and smiled as Breezy pranced inside the house.

Reggie wondered what it was like inside the house. He had heard stories, of course, but he had never been. Pigs were not allowed inside. The dog could go in, sometimes a cat would wander by and be invited, and once the old goat got confused and ended up in the farmer's upstairs linen closet. But no one had ever known a pig to set hoof inside. Reggie couldn't even imagine what it looked like in there, but he could imagine what it felt like, because he could hear the sounds. He could hear running and laughter, barking and the playful growling that accompanied the squeak of rubber toys. Reggie thought of the new word he had heard yesterday. *I wonder*, he thought, *is that what love sounds like?*

As Reggie listened more intently, he heard another sound coming from a different direction. This one was coming up the dirt road. It sounded vaguely like the farmer's truck, but not as rattling and clanky. He looked to the left and saw, coming around the big oak tree, a new thing with four wheels approaching the house. The driver looked a lot like the farmer, only younger. As this new machine came closer, it made a strange honking sound, then dust flew as it stopped abruptly by the front door. The farmer stepped out of the house, arms open wide, his smile even wider, and the young farmer unfolded himself from the contraption and embraced the older man.

"Oh," said Reggie to no one, "so that's the son." Breezy came bounding out next, running around the son's legs five times before they all went back inside. As soon as they disappeared, Reggie was overwhelmed by the feeling of being left out. There they all were, inside. Together. With that *love* thing. He heard talking. Then laughter. Talking again. He saw the big apple pie that was cooling in the kitchen window disappear. Clinking. Something scraped across wood. Sighs and murmurs of "mmmmm, that's good." And Reggie couldn't take any more. He had to get a look inside that house.

He went over to the shady corner of the pigpen, where the fence met up with the big tree. Reggie knew, and had known since we has a piglet, that if you held your head just right, held your breath just right, and pushed real hard with your back legs, a pig his size could just squeeze through a gap between the last fencepost and the tree, where the ground had gotten soft from rain puddles. Reggie did all these things, felt the gentle scrape and pressure of wood against his belly, and popped through the space, tumbling softly onto the grass on the other side. Although all the pigs knew about this hole, no one ever used it, because why would they? They had everything they needed in the pigpen. Pigs, it was understood, were not a very adventurous sort.

Reggie curved around the big tree and felt the sun shine down on his back as he left the shadows and headed for the house. Many times, he had watched as Breezy had come bounding out what he had called the "screen door." Reggie had noticed that you could see through it before it swung back and banged against the house. He had just heard that same bang when they had all gone into the house a moment ago, and by the sounds drifting out, he knew that the heavy inside door was still open. Maybe, if he was lucky, he might be able to sneak a look through it and finally see this place he had been dreaming about.

☙

Reggie, as quietly as a pig can be quiet, shuffled up the one small step onto the back stoop and inched his scruffy head closer to the screen door. The sounds and smells that wafted out to him made him a little bit woozy with delight, but soon he concentrated again on looking inside. He had to squint just right to focus beyond the wire mesh screen, but as he watched, the moving shapes began to take recognizable form. The farmer and his son were sitting at a table, talking, nodding their heads, and laughing, all while spooning heaping gobs of ice cream and apple pie into their mouths. Breezy stood between them on his hind legs, tongue hanging out, front paws on the table. It looked to Reggie as if Breezy was as much a part of the conversation as the two men. He nodded at the right times, wagged his tail, and Reggie was pretty sure that he even saw the dog laugh and shake his head at some kind of shared joke.

In a few minutes, the men rose from the table, laid their dishes in the sink, and, still talking, moved into a larger room beyond the kitchen. The farmer lowered himself into a contraption unlike anything Reggie had ever seen. At first, Reggie thought that the farmer had lost his balance and was accidentally falling into the jaws of a big, brown animal's gaping mouth to be swallowed up. He was about to squeal out a warning, but when the farmer sat down, the thing welcomed him by popping a small footrest out of its inner parts. The farmer's son walked to a longer, softer-looking version of the monster. "Where'd you get this couch, Dad?" the son asked.

"Old Lady Perkins was selling it in a yard sale."

"How much did you pay for it?"

"Well, nothing. She likes me."

"Hm. You still paid too much."

The son sat down on it anyway, and what Reggie saw next made time stand still. As soon as the son's weight settled onto the couch, Breezy leaped into the air and landed squarely in his lap. The son kept talking to the farmer, but while he was talking, he rubbed Breezy behind the ears, dug his fingers into Breezy's fur and scratched him, and sometimes he just gently stroked his coat with a gentle, smoothing motion. Breezy looked like he never wanted to move from that place.

So, thought Reggie, *that's what love looks like.*

Chapter 3

༄

Walk This Way

Reggie squeezed back through the fence gap and splooshed softly into the pigpen, completely lost in thought. His pig brow furrowed as he trudged over to his favorite corner, plopped into the mud that was being baked harder every minute, wriggled down into it as far as he could, and examined the problem as hard as he knew how. *Breezy*, he thought, *gets to go inside. Breezy gets fed, sits on soft couches, stays dry when it rains, cool in the summer, warm in the winter. He gets fresh, clean water and baths. Breezy*, he thought, *gets love.* The answer was simple. Breezy got all of these things because he was very pet-like. He looked around at the mud. He watched the other pigs rooting around the same old ground, gnawing the last kernel off an old corn cob, and snoring loudly in the sun while their ears twitched away a pesky fly. *It's time,* Reggie thought, *to trade up.*

☙

The screen door banged again, and Breezy came out of the house like a shot. He was a black-and-white blur, and as he ran, he looked back over his shoulder. The son smiled, yelled "Fetch!" and heaved a fuzzy, bright yellow ball far and high into the open field. After it came down and made one bounce skyward, Breezy launched himself into the air and grabbed it in his mouth. Then the dog ran back to the son, just as swiftly as he had run away from him, tore the ground as he circled him three times, dropped the ball at the son's feet, and crouched down, waiting, ready to burst out again, muscles coiled in anticipation. The son threw the ball again— except he didn't really, he just pretended to throw it. Breezy rocketed about ten dog lengths out, then, realizing he had been had, seemed thrilled at the joke and barked delightedly while chasing his tail in a circle. The son laughed at him, and threw the ball farther than last time. Breezy bounded after it, lost it in the tall grass for a moment, then barked again as he located it, retrieving and returning it just like before. Reggie backed away from the fence, closed his eyes, and recreated that game in his memory, noting all of the dog's movements and mannerisms. *I can do that,* he thought. *I can be pet-like, too, if that's what it takes.*

⨀

"Alright," Reggie said to no one, "let's fetch." There were no fuzzy yellow bouncy balls to be had in the pig pen, so he looked around for a suitable substitute. Jimmy Dean was absent-mindedly nibbling away at an apple core with just enough apple left on it, and Reggie decided that would do just fine. "Hey Jimmy," he called, "I need your apple for a minute."

"Get your own," replied Jimmy Dean. "I'm eating it."

"No, you're not," said Reggie, "you're just licking it. Let me use it for a minute. Please?"

"What do you need it for?"

"I'm gonna fetch it."

"You're gonna do what?"

"Fetch it."

"Oh," said Jimmy Dean, who didn't want to look like he didn't know what Reggie was talking about, which he didn't. "Come get it, then."

Reggie picked up the apple in his mouth and trotted back to the far end of the pig pen. He knew he had to have some room. He walked over to he corner where an old fence board had been knocked into the pen by the farmer's truck one day and had come to rest on top of an old branch that had fallen from the big oak tree in the corner. The piglets had found that if they balanced just right, they could get on each end of the board and one could go up when the other went down. And if one of them went down hard enough, the other pig could fly, at least for a second, which was something no one ever believed could happen. Reggie knew how this could work, but he needed a helper. He looked around the pigpen and finally spotted him, snoring and twitching in the sun in the biggest mud hole available.

"Hey, Tiny," called Reggie, "wake up. I need you for a second."

Tiny, who was not at all, didn't budge. "Hey!" yelled Reggie again. "Tiny! Get up!" Nothing. Reggie sighed, then walked over to the slumbering giant. This time he called to him in a sing-songy voice: "Ti-i-i-ny," he sang, "the truck is coming." Tiny still didn't open his eyes, but he did mutter something out of one side of his mouth.

"Nuh-uh," he said. "I can hear it when he starts it up."

"Well, since you're awake now," said Reggie, "come help me with something."

"I'm sleeping," he murmured."

"No, you're not. Not anymore. Come on, if you'll help me, I'll give you some of my share when the truck comes."

Tiny sighed loudly, making little mud bubbles pop up in front of his snout. "Oh, alright," he said.

22

After the big pig pushed himself upright, Reggie led him over to the old, fallen fence board. Carefully laying the apple core on the end closest to the end of the pigpen and pushing that end down to the ground, Reggie pointed himself away from it, crouched down as low as a pig can crouch, and said, "All you have to do is just fall down on this high end of the fence board with all of your weight at once."

Tiny looked at the board, which angled up from the ground almost to the middle of his belly, and said, "Just fall on it? That's it?"

"That's it," said Reggie.

"That's easy. That's almost like going to sleep. Ready?"

"Ready," said Reggie, who crouched a little lower.

Tiny pushed all of his weight over to one side, and tipped slowly over. At least it was slow at first. The further he tipped, the more his big round body picked up speed. He crashed onto the end of the board, the other end sprang up, and the apple core went soaring through the air down the length of the pigpen.

Pigs, though they look like cumbersome creatures, are not slow, as anyone who has chased a greased one already knows. Reggie shot down the muddy yard, past sleeping pigs and eating pigs, and staring pigs, watching the apple core with every step. The apple core reached the top of its arc and tumbled downward, right toward Reggie's open mouth. He judged where it would come down, lunged for it at just the right moment, and— missed it completely. The apple core landed with a thud in the mud, Reggie's front legs crossed over each other, and he half-slid, half-rolled right into the other end of the pigpen fence, his open mouth scooping up wet and baked mud all along the way.

"Ptooie!" he said, "Blech!" He spit out the mud, stood up, narrowed his eyes, and shouted to Tiny: "Again!"

Reggie tried again and again, until he was so tired and his mouth was so full of mud, that he decided "Fetch" must be an advanced pet-game. He would get there eventually, but maybe not today. Surely, though, all it would take would be dedication, concentration, and devotion. *It would come,* he assured himself. *Just work harder, and your pet-ness will show up eventually. Just a little more time. And practice. And more practice...*

Reggie moved on to more dog-like activities, certain that was what it took to be in the house with the farmer and his son. He tried to remember all the things Breezy did, and began to imitate him. He couldn't run in circles as fast as Breezy, and when he attempted to bark, all the other pigs stopped what they were doing and looked at him as if they expected him to cough up something strange and horrible. He stuck his tongue out like Breezy and panted, but it just made him lightheaded. Then he pretended that the mud all over him was soap and suds, and he shook like Breezy, which only made him dizzy, which, combined with the lightheadedness of panting, made him stagger three steps to the left and fall back into a mud puddle.

Soon, the other pigs noticed Reggie's unpiggish behavior and they gathered around to watch his "pet practice." "Hey, Reg," said Arbuckle, as he watched his friend try valiantly to wag his curly tail, "what in the wide world of mud are you doing?"

"I'm doing what all dogs do," he said proudly. "I'm being doggy."

"But you're not a dog," said Arbuckle.

"Says you," said Reggie.

Arbuckle snorted. "Yes, says me. And says your pig belly, your pig nose, your pink piggy ears, snorty piggy nose, and curly piggy tail, which, by the way, ain't never gonna wag."

"Nope," said Reggie, turning his snout up and away, and closing his eyes in an attempt to ignore the nay-sayer. "I may still look like a pig, but I choose to be a dog."

"Hmph," humphed Arbuckle. "How can you choose to be something you ain't?"

"Through careful observation, great discipline, and lots of practice, I will be a dog and will be treated like a dog, even if it kills me."

"Well," said Arbuckle, shaking his head as he sauntered away to find some cool mud, "if you try to chase the big old mean barn cat like he does, it just might."

Reggie refused to be dissuaded, and he pledged to spend even more time at dog practice. "I just have to try harder at being a pet," he said to himself. "If I'm ever going to live inside, I just have to!"

Chapter 4

೨൬

This Little Piggy
Learns A Lesson

Reggie stood absolutely still, and he was beginning to question his normally sound state of mind. The barn loomed before him, the tall red doors latched together but still swaying and swinging in the late evening summer breeze. There was no light beyond the gap between the doors, at least none that Reggie could see. One door eased toward him, making the gap wider. "Coooome iiiiiin," it creaked at him. "Nooooo, doooooon't," moaned its brother as it pulled the first one back, the latch keeping them together, twins in chains.

Reggie was more determined than ever to prove that he was as good a dog as— well, as a dog, and even though Arbuckle hadn't meant to, he had given Reggie an idea. *If I can face down the mean old barn cat*, he thought, *there would be no question of my pet-ness.* She lived in there, he knew. He had only seen her once or twice, but he had heard her hissing, her *pfffffting* when she encountered Breezy, and her mournful wailing when the moon was full, like a small child lost in the woods.

Malice was a big cat. No one knew how long she had been around, and she was never let into the house. She subsisted, apparently quite well, on mice and squirrels and other small animals unlucky enough to think that the barn would offer a measure of protection from predators. She only moved when she had to, and you never knew she was there until she was there.

Reggie smartly considered turning right around and pigtailing it to a mudhole, but he steeled his resolve and stepped toward the towering doors. The wind blew one of them forward. "Coooome iiiiin," it said again, and he scooted through the gap as the other futilely warned him from behind. Inside, the musty scent of hay swirled with the musky smell of horses. Reggie felt the gathering darkness settle, deep and cool, into his skin.

"Mmmmwell," he heard, a rumbling raspy voice, deeper than the darkness. "Mmmmmwho do we have here?" Reggie had heard that Malice's words always started from the lower parts of her hungry belly before they rolled out of her mouth with claws of their own. It occurred to him that her name might actually have been Alice before the first time she introduced herself.

Reggie made his insides taller. "My name is Reggie," he forced out, "and I am here to… to… well, I'm just here." The darkness moved a little, and began to take shape and stalk closer. "Mmmmmis that right?" it said.

"Yes, it is," said Reggie the Brave, "and I came to tell you to stop frightening all the other animals. There."

"My, mmmmmmy," purred Malice, though you would hardly call it a purr if it came from any other cat. "I don't think I have ever been so spoken to by a swine. Mmmmmnoo, I'm quite sure I haven't."

This isn't so bad, thought Reggie. "Well, get used to it," he proclaimed.

"Or what!" shouted Malice, suddenly behind him, her breath hot and prickly in his ear. Reggie whirled around almost in mid air. "Or… or I'll bark at you and chase you!"

Then the cat laughed, but there was no humor in it at all, and she sounded like she was up high in the rafters. "I'd certainly like to see that!" she said, right behind him again.

Reggie frowned. "Well, I'll do it!" he said. "And you won't like it! Not one bit!"

And then Malice was walking in a circle around him, and he was encompassed by *cat*, every part of him feeling it, front to back and all around, whiskers and tail and legs and back, brushing against him, drawing him into a tightening whirlpool of fur. As her huge head drifted past his face, he saw her eyes, one fierce green, the other dead and milky white, with a scar cutting directly above and below it. "Mmmmmand what makes you think you can frighten me, little sausage?"

"Because I have seen the farmer do it!" he said. Reggie wriggled out of her grasp, lifted one hoof, and flicked it at Malice. "Shoo!" he said, as loudly and deeply as he could, but it still sounded very much like a panicked squeal. "Shoo cat!" he said again. Malice looked genuinely confused for a moment. But only a moment. Then she began to tremble with laughter that started in her tail and made its way up to her jagged teeth.

"I ammmmmmm very much enjoying you," she said. "But not as much as I will be enjoying you in a bit." She flexed her claws.

"I've also seen Breezy run you off!" Reggie lowered his head a little, lifted his haunches, bared what little teeth he had, and tried, once again, to bark. It still came out as a squealy cough. He barked again, louder, but no better.

Malice stopped laughing. "Mmmmmmmm. I grow tired of you, Fun Size," she mewled. "You come in here, into my parlor, no bigger than a leftover piece of ham sandwich, and you think you can scare me with the farmer's words and the dog's demeanor? The farmer I know. The dog I know. But *who are you*?!?" The big cat leaped high into the air and came hissing down at Reggie, claws bared and slicing the darkening air. Reggie pedaled backward as fast as he could, turning quickly, just enough to save his face but not his hind quarters. Malice's razors tore through the skin of his left flank as he bolted for the swinging barn door.

And as he crashed through into the safety of the open air, Reggie could hear laughter behind him, and he could not tell if it was the barn door or the devil.

Chapter 5

The Chosen One

The next day, after nursing his cat scratches and completely exhausting himself with more frustrating pet practice, Reggie succumbed to the siren call of a much needed nap. He awoke in the mud in mid-afternoon to the sound of shoes scraping along the gravel outside the pen. He opened one eye and saw the farmer, the son, and Breezy coming his direction. "I know it sounds strange, Dad," the son was saying, " but I could sure use the company this summer. You know they say that having a pet helps your blood pressure stay low?"

"Oh, I don't mind, son," said the farmer, "you can choose any of the animals we have, I just don't get why you would choose one of *these*." The farmer motioned to the pig pen as they came to a stop and leaned on the top rail of the fence.

"Actually, I read an article recently that said that pigs are smarter than dogs." For the first time in a long, long while, Reggie saw the smile disappear from Breezy's face for a brief moment. Then he smiled again, as if to say, *Yeah, well, I know better.*

"Besides," the son continued, "pigs don't have sweat glands, so they really don't smell bad once you take them out of the pigpen and clean them up."

"Yeah, good luck with that," said the farmer. "Well, which one?"

Reggie's ears had caught the phrase "cleaned up," and thought about Breezy's bath. I wonder, he thought again, if I'm the pet, do I get a bath? *And does that lead...* he could hardly bear the thought of it... *to the inside of the house?* Just the prospect of being inside the house sent a tingly feeling up and down his spine. Reggie stood proudly, hurried over to the fence, stood right in front of the son, and looked up at him. The son smiled down.

"This one," he said.

❧

And just like that, Reggie's life was changed. The son unlatched the pigpen gate and Reggie slipped out before it had fully swung open, leaving clumps of dried mud on the post and the gate as he shot free.

Out of the dark of the old tree and into the bright sunshine, headed for he didn't know what, Reggie eyed the back door and pumped his little legs as hard as he could. Just before he reached the back porch, Breezy growled once and jumped in his path.

"Stop!" he barked.

"It's okay!" said Reggie. "The farmer's son said it's okay! I can come inside!"

"No, he didn't. Have you seen yourself? Look at all that mud! This house is clean and it stays clean. It is not a house for pigs."

Reggie looked down. Breezy had a point. Years of pigness had taken its toll on Reggie. Mud was wedged between his toes, packed into every crevice, clinging to a number of hairs, and when he concentrated, he could feel the dirt falling down deeper into his ears.

"But the son said…" Reggie began, not really knowing how he would finish.

"Said what?" broke in Breezy. "Said you were nice? A good pig? So what? He likes all of the animals on his farm, but they don't all get to come inside the house."

Reggie began to question what he had actually heard. Why had the son chosen him, if he would never be allowed in the house? What was the point? Was this just a cruel joke? All the excitement and anticipation that had surged through his spirit just moments ago were now just as quickly ebbing out of every pore, and he felt a little weak at the loss. Breezy's voice softened with his face, and he said, "I'm sorry, Reggie, but think about it. You're a pig. You are a great pig, but you're still a pig, through and through. Your mother is a pig. Your father was a pig. Your brothers and sisters are pigs. And pigs live in the pig sty. Not in the house. That's just the way it is. You see, as a dog, I have the right to say who comes in and out and…"

But no matter what Breezy said, the voice of the son saying, "This one" kept echoing over and over in Reggie's mind. That had to have meant something, it just had to. And as Breezy kept talking, and as Reggie's heart was sinking, a soft, tall shadow crept up over the steps of the back porch. As it covered Reggie, then Breezy, the dog fell silent. Reggie look up, blinked away a tear, and saw the son smiling down. Then he stooped low, scooped up Reggie, apparently with no thought as to how dirty he would get himself, rubbed him behind his right ear, and carried him over to where a tub of white, sudsy water glistened in the sun. It was the same tub where Breezy had been bathed, the same tub that had made countless animals clean before him, and probably would be used for countless more after, but for Reggie, at this moment, it was his bath, and his alone.

The cold water from the hose had warmed in the sun just enough to be comfortably cool. Reggie had no intention of struggling as the son set him gently down, past the soft crackle of breaking suds bubbles, and splashed him softly into the clear, perfumed ripples. The fruity smell of grapes and gardenias wafted up into Reggie's nostrils and he hoped it would stay there forever. *So*, he thought, *that's what love smells like.*

As the son gently moved the running hose over Reggie's little body, Reggie felt new life soaking into his skin. The only water he had ever felt was the rain that sometimes poured through the hole in the roof of his pighouse or dripped unexpectedly from the leaves of the big tree after a summer storm. But those were annoyances and unwelcome. This water, though, that ran down his sides in cleansing sheets, this water was like putting on a new skin. He looked down, and though he could still see his feet, the water was getting murky. The son laid the still-running hose in the water, then, with both hands, began to rub the soap into Reggie's leathery hide. And very soon, Reggie felt the years of mud and slop lose their grip and fall off into the water, as if they had been forced out by the love of the son, never to be seen again. Even as the dirt and earth fell away, he could see that it was being replaced by a new, pinkish clean, and he smelled more grapes and gardenias, not just in his nostrils now, but all over him. The son wrapped a cloth around his right hand and gently scooped his fingers down into the hollow of Reggie's crusty ears, loosening the layers of earth that had settled there and coaxing every grain of it up and out into the suds that now covered his head. As the dirt and mud came out with the suds, Reggie found that he could hear like he never heard before. And here is what he heard with his brand new ears: "Now, there's that beautiful little boy. I knew he was hiding in there somewhere. What a wonderful pig! My favorite pig in the whole world. Let's get you rinsed off and dried, and you can come in the house with me."

And Reggie thought, *Oh. So that's what love sounds like.*

When Reggie was fully scrubbed and rinsed, when all the residue of his previous life had been separated from his new one and he stood in the watery remains of who he had been before, the son lifted him up and out of the tub. As he was floating through the air on the way to the middle of a bright yellow towel, Reggie stole a last glance at the water. No suds left, no grapes and gardenias. The tub was now full of all of his days of slop, caked-on mud, pesky flies, and bits of chewed on apples and corn. *There is my old life,* thought Reggie, *and there it will stay.*

But he was wrong. The son set Reggie down in the center of the big fluffy towel, and as he vigorously rubbed the thirsty cloth all over him, Reggie saw the farmer pick up one side of the tub. He lifted it higher and higher, and as he did, the now brown water sloshed over the side, then waterfalled, then rushed out of the metal tub until it was a small brown river in the grass, a river that ran with great fury for about two feet, then just as quickly disappeared into the ground as if it had never been. *All of those years of mud and grime,* thought Reggie, *and now they are gone forever.* He liked the thought of that.

Next Reggie felt himself being warmly wrapped up in the towel, and once again his feet left the ground as the son picked him up and cradled him in his strong arms. Reggie watched out in front of him. They turned toward the house. One step toward the back door. Two steps. The farmer went ahead and held the door open with a smile, as the entrance grew larger in Reggie's vision. Reggie looked down and became aware of Breezy running circles around the son's legs, barking frantically, though Reggie could understand what he was saying: "Wait a minute! What are you doing? Are you sure you know what you're doing? That's a *pig*, for crying out loud! You can't bring a pig into the house! That is *my* house!"

And yet on they went. As Reggie was carried by the son across the threshold, the very air changed. The hot, humid air of the outside world became the cool, conditioned air of the house. The light changed from too bright to just right. The smells changed from decaying corn cobs in the mud to fresh fruit in a bowl and just-snapped beans in a bushel basket next to the kitchen table. The son set Reggie down, removed the towel, and knelt down in front of him so that now they were eye to eye. "Well," said the son, smiling, eyes twinkling. "This is your house now. Welcome home." Reggie heard the screen on the back door slam shut, just catching Breezy's tail in it, but Reggie didn't know if the dog's frightened yelp was because of his tail or because of what the son had just said.

The son stood and walked over to the big soft-looking couch that Reggie had seen through the screen door before. He sat down on it, looked at Reggie standing on the edge of the kitchen, slapped his hands on the top of his legs, and said, "Come here, boy! Come on up here and sit with me." Reggie began to trot across the floor, but Breezy flew past him like a bullet and leaped effortlessly off the floor and into the son's lap, turning quickly toward Reggie so that Reggie could see whose lap this really was. The son lovingly moved the dog aside onto the couch next to him. "Come on, Breezy," he said, "it's alright. I love you, too, but let's welcome the new little guy, okay?" Reggie continued across the floor, making a new sound, his cloven feet clomping on the hard wood in perfect rhythm with each other. He took a lesson from what Breezy had just done, gaining speed as he crossed the room, and at just the right second, Reggie pushed off of his feet with all his might, reached out with his front legs, and whumped right into the front of the couch, barely inches off the floor. *Well, that's great,* he grimaced. *I thought that now that I was inside the house that I could do all of the pet stuff just right. How can I ever reach the top of the couch?*

And even as the thought strode its way through his mind, his world changed again. "Oh my goodness," said the son, "bless your heart! I bet that didn't feel good." And the son leaned over, and with those same strong hands that carried him inside, Reggie was lifted up off the floor and set down affectionately in the son's denim-clad lap. "Now there," said the son, "that's better, isn't it? It's okay. You don't have to be able to get up here by yourself. I got you." And he rubbed Reggie behind the ears, pushed his fingers into Reggie's hide and scratched him, and sometimes he just stroked his pink piggy skin with a gentle, smoothing motion. And Reggie never wanted to move from that place.

So, Reggie thought, *this is what love feels like.*

Chapter 6

⁓

Getting To Know You

Reggie had just had the night of his life. Once, when he was very young, he had heard a bedtime story about a place where pigs were comfortable and pampered, and who slept where the air was always just the right temperature. The point of the story was clear, though: Reggie was never going to actually be one of these prized "show pigs," but at least he could dream about what that kind of life might be like. And he did dream. He dreamed about it so often, that on this day, when he woke up to the sound of the farmer's son humming a pleasant tune, and the feel of a strong hand gently rubbing his ears— instead of the musty smell of mud and the buzzing of pesky flies— he thought he was still dreaming. But as he slowly opened his eyes and took in the warm colors of the room around him and the softness of the couch cushions under him, he was amazed at where he found himself.

"Hey, you're awake!" he heard the son say. "How about some breakfast?" Now, "breakfast" was a word that Reggie had heard, too, but it wasn't a word from bedtime stories. It was a word from scary, don't-wander-away-from-home-or-this-will-happen-to-you stories. The older pigs told "breakfast" stories that were just too unbelievably horrible to be true, and the chickens wouldn't talk about it at all. "Come over here," said the son, "I have something for you."

He gently set Reggie down on the floor and he walked over to the kitchen. The son reached down, removed the lid from a large plastic bin, and with a bright metal scoop poured little round chunks of all colors and sizes into a big red bowl on the floor. Reggie trotted over to the bowl, tentatively pushed his nose into the mound, and looked up at the son. "Go ahead," he said, "it's for you." At this, Reggie, who just now realized how hungry he really was, dove into it, sucking in and swallowing the stuff at the same time. As he devoured it, he caught a glimpse of Breezy in the corner of the kitchen, looking not happy at all. The son reached down, rubbed Breezy's head, and said, "Oh, don't worry, boy, we still have all the dog food you can eat. You won't even miss what the little pig eats."

And as Reggie worked his way down to the bottom of the bowl, the son said, "I can't keep calling you 'little pig.'" He lowered himself down to the floor, crossed his legs, and moved his face closer. Between bites, Reggie was captured by the intensity of the son's gaze, and he stopped chewing. Their eyes connected, and it seemed as if the son was hearing words that weren't being said. The son moved his face even closer, looking way beyond Reggie's eyes, and before he knew it, Reggie had even stopped breathing. He didn't exactly know what he was waiting to hear, but he waited anyway. The son slowly smiled. Then he nodded his head. "I know," he said. "I know what I'll call you: Reggie. And one day, I'll tell you why that's your name."

⁂

After breakfast, Reggie explored his new surroundings. First, he snuffled along under the little ruffle on the bottom of the couch. After just a little bit of snuffling and a lot of sneezing, he moved on to the big, square, stone hole in the wall that still had ashes and charred wood in the bottom. Reggie knew that this was where the Farmer and his son built fires when the weather was cold. He remembered more than a few frigid nights in the chilled mud when he could see the light of the fire blazing happily in the house and hear the warm sounds of laughter and barking inside. It was still too much to believe that he would be there to see it and be warmed by it himself when the leaves fell again. But he made himself believe it anyway.

As Reggie wandered away from the fireplace looking for the next interesting thing, he heard a less-friendly-than-usual voice behind him. "Hey!" it said. Reggie turned to see Breezy sitting on his haunches, and he couldn't tell if the discomfort on the dog's face was from his sitting position or the new roommate.

"Hey," said Reggie.

Breezy didn't say anything for a moment, just stared at Reggie. Then he sighed, shook his head, and said, "Look, Reggie, I like you. Always have. We're friends."

"And…?" said Reggie.

"And I'm just trying to understand what's happening here. Don't get me wrong, I'm not mad at you or anything, but what are you doing here? What I mean is, why do the Farmer and his son need another pet in the house? I've been with them a long time, and I thought that I was doing everything they wanted me to do, but maybe I'm not. I've been trying and trying to think about how I must have disappointed them, but I can't come up with anything. I've worked hard, I've been loyal, I've played when they want to play, I've just rested at their feet when they were tired. I don't eat too much, I don't whine or howl at night,

I chase away the raccoons and the armadillos. I must be missing something. I wish I knew what I've done wrong."

"Wow," said Reggie. "I had no idea you had so much to do. I thought your life was just running around and being carefree."

"Well, sure," said Breezy, "that's part of it. But that's also part of my job! That's what pets do! Who knows what would happen if I stopped being a good pet? They might put me back out into the woods, and I've been there already. I'm not going back to living outside, all by myself again."

"What can I do?" asked Reggie.

"Nothing for me," said Breezy, "I'll just have to watch myself and try harder. I'll tell you one thing, though. You better watch yourself, too, or they might throw us both out and bring in somebody we've never even seen before! I'm going to work harder. I suggest you do the same."

"Thanks," said Reggie quietly. For the first time since he was brought into the house, he felt a little afraid. Breezy started to walk away, and then, without even turning his head, he said, "Oh, almost forgot. Welcome to the family."

Chapter 7

✎

No Place Like It

Reggie watched Breezy push the screen door open and scoot outside. As Breezy's paws hit the steps, he seemed to pick up his stride until he was directly on the farmer's heels. He looked back toward the house for a moment, and Reggie was struck by the stern look of concentration on the dog's face. Reggie got the distinct feeling that Breezy wasn't going to be nearly as fun as he had been up until now. He looked as if he had a serious job to do and nothing was going to stop him. It was a look that scared Reggie.

Reggie clomped over to the screen door, budged it open with his snout, and stepped out onto the little concrete porch. Right away, the inside smells of the house drifted away, and were replaced by the outside smells of the farm. Reggie had not even realized that he had slept all night without the smell of mud, slop, and other pigs in his nostrils. Now, though, those familiar scents drifted over to him, like wispy fingers, beckoning him to follow. They wriggled their way into his snout, and he sniffed the air, finding the old smell of musty mud and decaying vegetables somewhat appealing. He looked behind him into the house and took in the clean wood floors, the soft and comfy couch, the cool, conditioned air. He was very happy to be part of the family that lived here. Then he swiveled his head back around and saw the little piglets playing their launch-and-plop game again. They squealed with glee. He saw his mother asleep in the shade of the big tree. Tiny was digging in the dirt for some morsel of food that some other pig might not have finished. Arbuckle was stumbling out of a pighouse, obviously just waking up for the day. Arbuckle was not a morning pig.

"Hey, Arbuckle!" shouted Reggie, with a wide grin. "Look at me! Look where I am!"

Arbuckle squinted toward him, yawned wide, and scratched his belly with a hind leg. "You better get away from there," he said, "before the farmer sees you out of the pen. You're gonna get in trouble."

"Nuh-uh," said Reggie proudly, shaking his head from side to side. "I slept in the house last night!"

"No you, didn't," said Arbuckle, starting to fall asleep standing up.

"Yes, I did!," said Reggie firmly as he trotted over to the fence. "The son washed me, petted me, rocked me, and fed me! I'm one of the family now!"

"So what are you doing over here?"

"What do you mean?"

"I mean, if you live in the house now, what are you doing standing in the mud?"

Reggie had not even realized that he had left the soft, green grass of the yard and now had mud squishing up between his toes. "I can be here if I want," he said.

Arbuckle gave a little shrug. "If you say so."

"I can!" replied Reggie loudly.

Arbuckle turned to amble away. "Whatever," he said. "Just if you're one of them now, you've probably already forgotten how to be a pig."

What? thought Reggie. *Forgotten how to be a pig? What does that mean? I'll show him that I am still just a regular pig.* With a frown of determination, he squeezed himself between the fence post and the big tree, the rough feel of bark rubbing into his bristles again, until he plopped forward into the familiar pig sty. "Hey, Tiny!" he yelled. "Find me that apple core!"

❧

For the next three and a half hours, Reggie was, in fact, just like a regular pig. He ran through the deepest mud, ate the rottenest fruit, squealed the squealiest squeals, snorted the snortiest snorts, and took the longest naps he had ever had, forcing himself to lay there until new layers of wet dirt and clay baked themselves onto his skin. His heart sank a little, though, as he realized that he no longer smelled like grapes and gardenias, he no longer glistened from the soap and shampoo, and if he wasn't mistaken, his hearing was becoming muffled again as new clumps of earth fell into the now available spaces in his ears.

Confident that he had thoroughly proved his pigness without question, though, Reggie rose from his crackly mud bath, squeezed back through the opening by the tree, and headed back toward the house. It had been a hard morning of making sure his friends knew that he hadn't changed, and now he was looking forward to the conditioned air and continuing his nap on the farmer's new couch. But just as he placed his front hoof on the porch, Breezy, as if from thin air, landed on all fours in front of him, and for a moment, Reggie thought that he saw his friend baring his teeth at him.

"No!" barked Breezy. "You cannot go in there!"

"But I can," answered Reggie. "Remember yesterday? I'm part of the family now. Remember?"

"Oh, I remember," said the dog. "I remember that the son, for reasons that I *still* do not understand, bathed you, dried you, picked you up and brought you inside."

"Thank you," said Reggie, starting to edge around him. Breezy sidestepped into his way.

"But look at you now," he said. "You are a mess! Don't tell me you think you deserve to go back into the house. Look at how clean it is in there! I'm afraid you have done it, now, Reggie. You had a chance at the good life, but, as I suspected, you are still just a dirty, smelly, slop-breath pig!"

Reggie was frozen in place. He couldn't believe what he was hearing from his friend, but he couldn't deny it either. His brown eyes felt warm and wet as tears welled up in them. What had he done? Had he really thrown all of that love away just to prove something to a bunch of pigs who still wallowed in the garbage? What was he thinking?

Reggie hung his head and a single, large round tear fell from his face and splashed lightly on the porch. "I see," he said.

Breezy gently put a paw on Reggie's shoulder and his voice now became as soft as Reggie remembered it. "It's not really your fault," he said, "it's just who you are. You can't stop being who you are, Reg. You are a pig, and you'll always be a pig. And there's nothing wrong with that. It's just that pigs like you can't really hope to ever live in the Farmer's house."

Reggie felt his chest heave a little and his knees got weak. "I... I'm sorry," he said, softly. He didn't know what else to say. The day had suddenly become darker, and he turned to make his way back to the old pig pen. Suddenly, the thought of more mud, more rotting food, more flies… now it all sounded terrible. As he stepped away from the porch, he felt the weight of the day's dirt, as if all the mud in the world had wrapped itself around him, and he never felt heavier in his life.

But in that one, trembling step, he bumped against something. It was long, and blue, and hard and soft at the same time. Reggie looked up from the ground and saw that he had bumped into the Farmer's son's leg, with the soft blue jeans giving off the scent of laundry soap that Reggie thought he would never smell again.

"Where are you going, little guy?" The son said. Reggie looked up, but he couldn't see the man's face, since the sun was right behind his head. The day had not really gotten darker, after all. In the middle of Reggie's sadness and shame, the shadow of the son was covering him. The son knelt down and began to inspect Reggie's newly clogged ears. "I saw you playing in the mud this morning," he said. "You were having quite a time. But you want to come back in, don't you?" he said. He scraped a piece of hardened clay off Reggie's snout with his thumbnail. "You know I can't let you inside again like this, don't you?"

Breezy stepped over behind the son, so that Reggie could see him, and wore a look that said, "That's too bad," and "I told you so" at the same time. Reggie took a step to leave the porch and go back to the pen, but as soon as his foot left the concrete, he felt himself being lifted into the air. "Come on," said the son, "it's ready."

And once again, Reggie was carried through the bright morning air in the arms of the son, to where a fresh bath waited in the old metal tub. Glistening bubbles popped, and grapes and gardenias greeted him again as he was lowered gently into the water. "I ran your bath when I saw you getting muddy again." The son ran his soapy hands over him again, but this time he didn't have to scrub as hard or as deeply. This was just one day's worth of dirt, not a whole lifetime's. "Reggie, I hope you will learn quickly that I'll always wash away your dirt and grime, because you are part of the family now. I'm not going to let your sliding back into the pig pen keep you out of the house that you belong in. However," he said with a smile, "life will be a lot easier for me and you both if you will just stay out of the mud."

And as the water washed his outside, something else washed his inside. It felt like his heart moved a little in there, and Reggie knew that nothing the pig pen offered him could ever compare to the wonders of life with the son inside the Farmer's house. Staying clean suddenly seemed easier than he had ever imagined it would be.

Chapter 8

༄

The Long Run

Reggie woke slowly the next morning, becoming more and more aware of the soft and fluffy feel of his new bed. It looked just like Breezy's dog bed, but since Reggie was a pig, this was obviously a pig bed. It was round, and deep, and cozy, and Reggie wondered if house animals were allowed to sleep all day long.

He could hear sounds outside the kitchen screen door, and every once and a while, he would catch a glimpse of Breezy bounding anxiously along with the Farmer, right on his heels, eager to prove that he could be a great help in gathering eggs, or feeding the chickens, or milking the cows. Reggie had never seen his friend work this hard before, but Breezy was determined to prove his worth and "earn his keep" as he called it, and Reggie hoped that he wasn't the cause of this newfound enthusiasm. He also hoped it wasn't contagious. In a moment, Reggie heard a noise, heavy but soft, and he looked up to see the son coming down the stairs, skipping two and three stairs at a time. He was dressed in a shirt with no arms, and on his feet were shoes like Reggie had never seen. They were bright blue and yellow, and they reminded him a little bit of the tires on the Farmer's car. *Those must be human tires*, he thought.

The son moved swiftly into the kitchen, where he began to make his own breakfast. Just the thought of what that might be sent a shudder through Reggie, and whatever it was, he absolutely didn't want to be anywhere near it. All thoughts of longer sleep vanished in an instant, and Reggie bolted out of his bed, slid across the kitchen floor, and blasted out of the screen door before he saw something that he would never get out of his head. Now, standing in the bright morning sun, Reggie looked over to his old home, the pig pen, and saw the other pigs stirring around, starting to play, and plopping over in the mud to keep cool in the quickly rising heat. Even though it was a bit appealing, Reggie knew better than to get muddy again. Who knew how many times the son would be willing to bathe him before he decided it was enough? No, Reggie wouldn't risk his new status in the family just for a few muddy drops of nostalgia. In fact, he considered that he might just have a duty to the other pigs to tell them how they might learn to be chosen as house animals, too. He didn't exactly know what he had done to earn the privilege, but he was sure he could identify it if he thought about it long enough. So, Reggie sauntered over to the pen, still proudly smelling of grapes and gardenias, and called out to the pigs.

"Hey, you guys!" he yelled. "Come here for a second!"

It took a few minutes, but eventually, most of the pigs (not all of them) wandered over to the fence where Reggie stood, head held high and hooves together.

"As most of you know," he began, "I am now an animal of the house. In fact, the Farmer and his son have called me a member of the family." He didn't know what kind of response he was waiting for, which was good, because he received none. "I used to be just like you," he continued, "rooting around in the dirt, splooshing in the mud, swatting at flies with mud-covered ears." As if on cue, a fly buzzed right into Arbuckle's right ear, and he shook his head and flicked it away.

"So?" said Arbuckle when the fly had vacated his ear.

"So, look at me now! Clean, fed, cooled by air that comes out of the wall, and with a nice, soft bed of my own, out of the rain, right next to the couch."

"So?" said Arbuckle again, quickly losing interest.

"So, don't you want to be like me? Don't you want to have what I have?"

Some of the pigs looked at each other, then one of the newer ones, Hamilton, shrugged his shoulders a little. "I guess so," he said. "Sure. What do we have to do?"

Reggie hadn't thought quite that far ahead yet. "Well," he said, "you have to do enough pet things to get the Farmer's attention. I'm sure that's what I did." He kept thinking. "And look at me! You have to get clean, too. Being clean is what gets you into the house." He thought some more. "And you have to not eat slop anymore!" At this, at least four of the eight or nine that had gathered just turned and walked away.

"Forget that," they said with a huff. "Eating slop is what we do. We were born for it."

"Wait!" cried Reggie. "There is more to eat than just slop!" But they didn't come back. They didn't even act like they had heard him. Reggie looked at the ones that were still there. "Listen," he said, "when it's time for breakfast…"

Two of the sows screamed and one fainted.

"No! It's not like that!" Reggie objected. But no one could hear him over the commotion of reviving one sow and trying to stem the sobbing of the other two. Soon, Arbuckle was the only one left at the fence while everyone else tried to resume their day, which was now much weirder than it had begun. Arbuckle shuffled over to the fence.

"Look, Reggie, I'm happy for you. Really, I am. But I don't think you should be coming over here trying to change us. Besides, if you're a pig of the house now, how come you don't go running with the son?"

"Running?" said Reggie.

"Yeah. Look." Arbuckle gestured with his head and Reggie followed his gaze to where the son had just emerged from the house in his blue and yellow foot tires, and Breezy was now running around the son in a blur, obviously knowing what was about to happen. Reggie trotted over to the blur and called out to his old friend.

"Hey, Breezy!"

The dog slowed a little, but was still bouncing excitedly. "What?"

"What's 'running'?"

Now Breezy stopped, not at all out of breath. "It's what we do every day!" he said. "Haven't you noticed?"

"Guess I was sleeping in," said Reggie.

"Well," said Breezy, "every morning, the son comes outside, and we take off down the driveway, down the dirt road, across the empty pasture, through the woods, and then back again. It's fun!"

"Really?" asked Reggie. "Doesn't sound like fun. Sounds exhausting. What's so fun about it?"

"Are you kidding? That's our *us* time! Just me and the son, running and running, breathing the fresh air, watching the leaves change colors. And he talks to me! Sometimes he sings to me while we're running. He throws things that I bring back, he chases me, I chase him. It's fun!"

"Oh," said Reggie, "I see." But he didn't see. It still sounded exhausting, but he knew that time spent with the son made the son see him as a better pet. Breezy himself said that they had both better work harder at being good pets, so obviously, this "run" thing is a must. Reggie knew better than to ask Breezy if he could come, too. He knew what his answer would be. So he just waited.

The son had been a few feet away, bending, moving, and pulling his arms and legs behind him and holding them there. Reggie sure hoped he didn't have to do that. Soon, the son whistled at Breezy, and they both trotted out to the driveway. When they reached the mailbox, Reggie started out after them. Pigs, it is well known, can trot very well. He stayed a little ways behind them, and decided this run thing might not be so bad.

"C'mon, Breeze," said the son, "let's turn it up." The man and the dog burst forward on the dirt road. Pigs, it is also known, are very fast, too, but only for short distances. Reggie took off like a shot. What is not so well known about pigs is that they can't keep their heads from moving up and down when they run. Less than a minute into the run, Reggie got dizzy, his hooves slid on the soft dirt, and suddenly there he was, tumbling, first through the air, then through the tall grass. He let out a high-pitched squeal of fear and surprise as he rolled into the ditch beside the road.

"Hey," he heard the son call. "Reggie? Is that you?"

The son turned around, ran over to Reggie, and gently picked him up out of the ditch. "What are you doing here?" he said. "You don't have to do this. I don't expect you to be able to keep up with me here." He laughed a gentle laugh, then rubbed Reggie between the ears. "You're just not designed for it, little fella!"

❧

Reggie sulked in his pig bed the rest of the day. Whenever the Farmer, or the son, or Breezy came into the room, he pretended to be asleep. But he was thinking. *I will do it,* he told himself. *Tomorrow, when the run starts, I will keep up. I'll prove that I am as good a house pig as anyone could ever want. They'll see.*

❧

The next morning, Reggie was already fully awake when the son came down the stairs. Reggie made himself stay in the room while the son had breakfast and he ate his pig food. As it turned out, there was nothing to be afraid of. The son just poured something tan into a round dish, poured some of the cow's milk over it (which the cows did not mind at all), and ate it with a small, round shovel.

Then it was outside, the moving and bending again, the whistle, and they were off. Reggie kept up with them pretty well, and in a moment, the son looked down at him, smiled, shook his head, and kept running. Breezy was already way ahead, trying to show how much faster he was than a pig.

By the time they reached the end of the old dirt road, Reggie was out of breath. He had never run this far in his life, an hoped he never would again. He didn't intentionally let the son and Breezy get further ahead, but when he saw it happening, it became a plan. Maybe he could make it look like he had run the whole way, just behind and out of sight. Breezy had said that they finished by coming out of the woods. This just might work. *It has to work,* he thought. *I'm dying here.*

When the son and the dog turned off the road to run across the empty pasture, Reggie made his move. He quickly doubled back, slowed to a trot, and went back down the dirt road. When he got back to the farm, he ran around behind the house so that the other pigs couldn't see him, around the far side of the barn, and carefully made his way into the thicket at the edge of the woods. He lay down, as close to the ground as he could get, and listened for the runners.

⚜

Reggie woke with a start, trying to remember where he was and why he was there. Just then, the son and Breezy came crashing through the woods at full speed, just a little ways from where Reggie lay hidden. The son was laughing, the dog was barking, and as soon as they passed him, Reggie charged out of the thicket and joined in the cheers, grunting, gronking, squealing. The two others stopped in their tracks and looked back at him. Breezy looked a little confused and angry at the same time. The son walked over to Reggie, knelt down, scratched him behind his left ear, and said, "Well, there you are. So. Did you have a good run?" Then he quickly closed and opened one eye. Reggie had no idea what that was about.

Yes, thought the little pig. *They bought it!*

⚜

Later that evening, after supper and a little music at the piano, the son sat on the couch and patted his lap with one hand and the seat next to him with the other. Breezy bounded up onto the couch cushion, and Reggie trotted over to the son's feet. The son leaned over, lifted Reggie up off the floor and into his lap as he was now doing every night, and Reggie rolled over so that he could rub the little pig's belly.

A few minutes later, just as Reggie was drifting off to sleep, the son leaned close in and whispered in his pink piggy ear. "I know," he said. Reggie looked up at him. "I know you didn't run with us today." Reggie didn't understand all the words, but he knew what was being said. What surprised him, though, was that the son was smiling as he said it. "It's alright," he said. "I love you just like you are, for exactly who you are. You don't have to impress me, little one. Do you want to know why I chose you? For this," he said, as he picked Reggie up in both arms and brought him close to his face. The son lovingly pressed his cheek up against Reggie's chubby pig cheek, held him against his chest a little closer, and said, "Just for exactly this."

Then the son held him out a little, right in front of his face, and Reggie found himself captured by those intense eyes again. The son spoke, his voice gentle and strong. "I'll tell you something else," he said. "I'll tell you why I named you Reggie. You think you're just a regular pig, but you are so much more than that. 'Reggie' is short for Regulus— Latin for 'little king.' And that's what you are now. You're a prince in this house."

Chapter 9

༄

The Story Of The Rest

Reggie couldn't remember ever having a better sleep. He woke slowly, gently, aware of his steady breathing, his brain and his eyes slowly rising together to meet the day. Even before he knew it was there, he could feel a smile on his little pig face, as if it had rested there with him all night long. Something had moved in him last night, not the usual movement of food through his belly, but just as real and even more satisfying.

Last evening, while being held in the son's lap, Reggie tried to figure out what he was feeling. He was as sure as he had ever been about anything, that the son knew that he had only pretended to run with him, yet he wasn't angry. How could that be? Shouldn't he at least be disappointed? Shouldn't Reggie be punished for his deception? And yet, the son just held him, and sang songs to him, and smiled at him, and rubbed him behind his piggy ears for a long time. And somehow, in a moment that seemed to slow down and grow brighter, Reggie realized something that was too good to be true, but had to be true anyway. In that moment, Reggie knew, to the very middle of his little pig heart, that the son loved him, no matter what. He loved him even though he couldn't run the whole way. He loved him, even if he couldn't play fetch. He loved him when he couldn't jump on the couch. He loved him when he got dirty. He loved him when he was making him clean again. He loved him when he was awake. He loved him when he was asleep. It occurred to Reggie in that slow moving moment, that he had not done one single thing to earn the son's love. He just loved him because he had chosen to.

And sometime in the night, as Reggie lay in his little round bed, something settled over him like an invisible warm blanket, and kept settling until it went all the way through him. For the first time in his life, Reggie knew that his heart was safe. This was his home. He didn't do anything to earn his place in it, and as amazing as it sounded, he couldn't do anything to be thrown out. Somehow, Reggie knew that no matter what he did, he was now and forever an inside pig.

❧

Reggie sauntered over to his bowl and found that for some reason, his food tasted even better. His water tasted even cleaner. The day was just brighter wherever he looked. He finished his breakfast, walked to the screen door, nosed it open, and stepped out onto the little porch. He closed his eyes, felt the sun on his face, and made full use of his prominent pig nose, breathing in all the fresh morning air that he could fit in his lungs, then slowly letting it out with a contented sigh. When he opened his eyes, he saw a big round head with one dead eye glaring at him from the gap between the barn doors. But whatever had changed in Reggie during the night, it brought with it a fierce knowledge that he had nothing to fear. Somehow, he knew that if he wanted to command Malice to leave, it would be just as good as if the son was chasing her away himself. What's more, Malice seemed to realize it, too. She frowned, lowered her head, and retreated slowly back into her darkness.

"Ahem," someone said near him. Reggie turned to see Breezy standing beside him with his head cocked to the side as is so often typical with dogs when they are curious.

"Morning!" said Reggie.

"Yes, it is," said Breezy. "What are you so happy about?"

"I feel… I don't know. Rested."

"Well, sure," said the dog, "you just slept all night."

"No, that's not it," said Reggie. "It's more than that. Deeper, somehow."

"What do you mean, 'deeper'?"

Reggie walked down off the porch and stood facing Breezy on the dewy grass. "Well," he said, "I feel peaceful. Like I don't have to be anything special, just me, and it's okay. You know… rested."

"No, I don't know," snapped Breezy, "I don't have time to rest! I have things to do, because I have to keep working if I want to stay in the house, and I suggest you try making yourself more useful, too!"

"But why?"

"Why? Why?!?" Breezy ran around twice in a tight circle like he was chasing his tail. "Because that's why we were brought inside, Reggie! To be useful! If you and I don't stay busy, the farmer and his son will find someone else who will do the job!"

Reggie pondered it for a moment. He almost believed that Breezy might be right, but his rested middle wouldn't let him. "I don't think so," he said gently.

"You don't think so! Well, what do you know about it, little pig?!? You just got plucked out of the muddy clay, washed in the tub, and set on the couch! You never knew what it was to be tossed out of a pickup truck by the side of the road, just to wander in the woods and scrounge for every bite, your stomach eating away at your insides until you found something slow enough that you could kill and eat! I made my own way, Reggie. And when I showed up on this farm, I made my own way here, too. I herded the pigs. I chased away the foxes. I made myself useful! And THAT is why I got brought inside! That's why I get fed every day. That's why I have a bed at night. That's why I get bathed, brushed, and petted!"

"No," said Reggie, "I think you've got it backwards. You once told me the story of when you showed up here for the first time. I want to hear it again. What was it like?"

"I was scared, you know that! I didn't know if these people were as bad as the ones I had already known."

"Did you run right up to the farmer, bouncing and wagging your tail?"

"No…"

"You hid, didn't you? Over there, just inside the woods. And you watched. Then what?"

"You know the story…"

"Tell me anyway."

"When it was dark, I snuck up to the garbage can and ate what I could. But I knocked it over. The porch light came on, and I panicked. I ran the wrong way, though, and was trapped in the chicken coop."

"And who came out?"

"The farmer came out. He saw where I had run, and he came over and found me in the corner, shivering."

"And what did he do, then?"

"He… he spoke to me. Softly. And he kneeled down with his hand out. There was food in it. It smelled good."

"Let me take it from here. And even then, you were still scared, but even hungrier. So he moved a little closer. Then you moved a little closer. And he smiled. And you stepped toward him. You ate what was in his hand as he rubbed you behind the ears. Right?"

"Yes…" Breezy laid down on the cool morning grass, remembering.

"Then you followed him to the porch where he fed you until you were full. And as he stroked your fur, he saw how matted and dirty it had gotten from your time in the woods. So he bathed you, right then and there. Your first real bath. And he brushed out the tangles, and dried you with a big, fluffy towel. Then what, Breezy?"

Breezy started to speak, but a tiny whimper arrived before the words. He was starting to cry a little. "Then… then he took me inside and made a bed for me out of pillows. And he laid down on the floor next to me and slept there with his hand on my back, all night."

Reggie let it be quiet between them for a moment as Breezy drifted back in time. Then he spoke. "Don't you get it?" he said. "The farmer doesn't feed you and bathe you and pet you and love you because of what you do for him. He did all those things before you ever did anything for him. Breezy, you are the farmer's dog because he chose you. You didn't get into this family because you earned it! Neither of us did! You belong here, Breezy, and you always will, no matter what you do, for one reason— because he has adopted you. Same as me."

Breezy lay there a moment longer. He sighed, a long, steady sigh. He looked up at Reggie. "I feel it," he said.

"Feel what?"

"That 'rest' thing you were talking about." Then, looking at Reggie with the eyes of a friend again, he said, "I like it."

A hint of a cool breeze from the coming autumn fluttered in the morning air. And the people who say that animals can't smile— well, they weren't standing there that day, as the sun rose higher over Far Away Hill.

PART 2

Chapter 10

Here Comes The Son

Brandon was raised on a dairy farm in the Midwest. When he was five years old, Brandon's mother and father divorced. It was a bitter and ugly parting, and in the aftermath, Brandon's mother hated him because he looked just like his father. This was not supposition on Brandon's part, for his mother told him this was the case. Although Brandon had older brothers and sisters, his mother forced him to sleep out in the barn with the animals. So, at the tender young age of five, Brandon would be banished to the barn every evening, left to find comfort by curling up next to the heat lamps that were there to keep the chickens warm at night. Every morning, Brandon's mother would put his bowl of oatmeal outside the back door, on the stoop, and he would eat like the dogs ate.

During his teenage years, a friend invited Brandon home with him one day, and that friend's family took him in, where Brandon would live and find out what love really is for the next three years. During that time, the friend's father asked Brandon to describe his most lasting impression of that bleak period of his childhood. "Sometimes," Brandon said, "in the early mornings, just before dawn would break, I would wake up and see the light come on in the kitchen window. And then, on some of those occasions, when I worked up the courage, I would sneak up to the house and look in the window, where I would see my mother putting out the breakfast plates and setting the places for my brothers and sisters. And every time," he said, "I hoped with all my heart that she would set a place for me. And she never did."

❧

Human history is Brandon's story. It is the story of mankind seeing the light and the life of God, and trying with everything he's got to find a way back into the house. It is the deeply ingrained knowledge in every heart that once, we had a place at the table, but now, because of sin, we are stuck sleeping in the barn, knowing that someone has made it inside, but not us. We seem to see others who must be sons and daughters feasting at the table of life, and we know there must be a way in, but alas, we are only orphans, and the family table does not belong to us. Of course, God is not a bitter and hateful parent, but because we have become so locked in to a performance mentality, we treat Him, and ourselves, as if He is.

Then comes the glorious dawn of the gospel, and we are told that the privilege of becoming a child of God is a gift, and cannot be earned. And for those who are willing to believe and receive that good news, we are adopted into the family of God, not by our deserving works, but because of His own love for us. (Romans 8:15-17, Ephesians 2:8-9) And all the children of God live in confidence and peace, enjoying for all their days the wonderful blessings of knowing God as Father. And yet…

❧

And yet, many Christians still live their lives as if they are trying to get back in the house and earn a place at the table. "How can I get God to meet my needs?" "What is the magic formula for prayer that makes God act?" "Which Scriptures can I quote to ensure that I get the blessings that have been promised to me?" "What must I do to really experience the benefits of being a child of God?" Orphan questions, all of them. But to the one who understands the reality of sonship, none of these questions need ever be asked.

HERE COMES THE SON

It is, in reality, a simple thing to distinguish the difference between the heart of an orphan and the heart of a son or daughter (for the sake of this book, we will use the term "son" generically to represent both male and female). A son is one who knows that three main aspects of life are his, guaranteed simply by the fact that God is his Father. Those things are:

1) Provision
2) Protection
3) Promotion

A son is one who is at least learning that if God is his Father, then God can be trusted to provide for him, protect him, and promote him in the Kingdom, in His timing. Seeing these three things as the basic inheritance of every child of God, the Bible then comes alive when read through these lenses. Suddenly, Jesus' words on the Mount of Olives begin to make sense, not as a command, but an illustration of what it means to be under the care of the Father:

"This is why I tell you: Don't worry about your life, what you will eat or what you will drink; or about your body, what you will wear. Isn't life more than food and the body more than clothing? Look at the birds of the sky: they don't sow or reap or gather into barns, yet your heavenly Father feeds them. Aren't you worth more than they? Can any of you add a single cubit to his height by

worrying? And why do you worry about clothes? Learn how the wildflowers of the field grow: they don't labor or spin thread. Yet I tell you that not even Solomon in all his splendor was adorned like one of these! If that's how God clothes the grass of the field, which is here today and thrown into the furnace tomorrow, won't He do much more for you-you of little faith? So don't worry, saying, 'What will we eat?' or 'What will we drink?' or 'What will we wear?' For the idolaters eagerly seek all these things, and your heavenly Father knows that you need them. But seek first the kingdom of God and His righteousness, and all these things will be provided for you. (Matthew 6:25-33)

So, in light of what is automatically ours by virtue of the fact that God is a good Father, Jesus does not command us not to worry, he gives us a good reason not to *have* to worry. This is illustrated just previously to Matthew 6, when, in Matthew chapter 4, Jesus demonstrates the difference that a secure knowledge of sonship makes in our lives.

Then Jesus was led up by the Spirit into the wilderness to be tempted by the Devil. After He had fasted 40 days and 40 nights, He was hungry. Then the tempter approached Him and said, "If You are the Son of God, tell these stones to become bread." But He answered, "It is written: Man must not live on bread alone but on every word that comes from the mouth of God. "Then the Devil took Him to the holy city, had Him stand on the pinnacle of the temple, and said to Him, "If You are the Son of God, throw Yourself down. For it is written: He will give His angels orders concerning you , and, they will support you with their hands so that you will not strike your foot against a stone. " Jesus told him, "It is also written: Do not test the Lord your God. " Again, the Devil took Him to a very high mountain and showed Him all the kingdoms of the world and their splendor. And he said to Him, "I will give You all these things if You will fall down and worship me." Then Jesus told him, "Go away, Satan! For it is written: Worship the Lord your God, and serve only Him. " Then the Devil left Him, and immediately angels came and began to serve Him. (Matthew 4:1-11)

We must look at the key phrases of sonship: "IF YOU ARE the Son of God…" (emphasis added). Satan is directly attacking Jesus' sonship. Many automatically interpret that as "If you are really divine, then prove it by doing something miraculous." This interpretation does not hold all the way through, though, as the last temptation is not about convincing Jesus to do something supernatural. Satan already knew who Jesus was, he needed no proof of His divinity. Each temptation, though, is a direct challenge to Jesus' confidence in the Father's provision, protection, and promotion. "I know you're hungry," he seems to say. "If you really are a son, surely God would not want you to suffer, so go ahead and make these stones into bread." Jesus' response? "It is precisely BECAUSE I am a son, that I am confident that my Father will not be late in His provision for me. I can wait. I have no need to prove my sonship. Instead, I will trust my Father to provide for me, to feed me when He is good and ready."

So satan moves on to the next area. "If you really are a Son, then prove it by demonstrating the Father's protection for you. Throw yourself off this high place and see what He does." Jesus' response? "It is precisely BECAUSE I am confident in my sonship, that I have no need to prove that the Father protects me. I just trust Him. He will protect me when He knows I need it, and right now I don't need it."

And the last: "If you are really a Son, then surely your Father would want you to run things. Bow down to me now, and you can run things right away." Jesus last response? "BECAUSE I am confident in my Father's love for me and in the benefits of my sonship, I can trust that He will promote me in His way and in His time. I have no need to promote myself, I need take no shortcuts. I'm going to have all of those kingdoms anyway, but I will have them when the Father decides, and not before. I can wait."

"Then the Devil left Him." Nothing defeats the power of temptation in our lives like the security of sonship. Both in a spiritual sense, and in the natural, in our own families, a son who is secure in the love

of his father knows that the father will provide for him. Those children have no need to scrounge for their daily bread. Sons know that their father will protect them. They sleep safely in his house, without worry about threats from without or within, because their father is watching over them. And sons know that their father will promote them. Every good father wants his children to surpass his success. The children of these fathers know that he is watching for every opportunity to help them achieve their highest potential and significance in life, and they know that he will spare no expense, even at the cost of his own life, to make that happen.

Orphans, though, live without that security. They know that if they are to eat today, it is up to them to find their food, and hold on to it so that no one else takes it away. If they are to be safe, they must provide their own security and keep a watchful eye out for themselves. If they are to achieve anything in life, they must take advantage of every opportunity to promote themselves and to sabotage the promotion of anyone who gets in their way.

The great tragedy of our day is that we are a people who claim to be sons, but we live like orphans. We preach and declare that God is our Father, yet we spend our energy and our time making sure that all of our bases of provision are covered. We say we trust God, but when we have a need, we worry ourselves sick and go to every length to meet our own needs, and then try to give God praise for it. When we are threatened, we lash out to protect ourselves. When attacked, when mistreated, we get defensive and do everything we can to make sure that everyone knows our side of the story. We protect ourselves and our reputations at all cost, even the cost of broken relationships. And when it seems that others "less deserving" than we are, get promoted around us or before us, we fume, we complain, and scheme and manipulate in order to make sure we get what is rightfully ours. We cannot rejoice when others are promoted, and we secretly are glad when others fail.

An even greater tragedy is that we are led by the same kind of people, both spiritually and culturally. In the Church, we as pastors have merely been Head Orphans in the orphanage, spending our lives trying to make people into better behaved orphans. We have secured our own provision with no thought of our Father's love for us, we have defended our positions, our theologies, and our reputations with venom and vehemence, thinking that our Father wanted us to do so, and we have promoted ourselves and our ministries in competition to our brothers, confident that we deserved to be the biggest and best. And we are still just looking in the kitchen window, trying to earn a way back into the house in which we already belong. We long to be invited to the table, unaware that there has always been a place with our name on it, waiting for us to simply trust that all we need is already ours by virtue of the goodness and love of our Father.

Culturally and politically, things are no better off. In any organization, and in any realm, spiritual or natural, there is nothing more dangerous than an insecure leader. Insecure leaders are prone to make critical decisions for all the wrong reasons: self-promotion, need for affirmation, the need to feel significant, fear of losing financial security, and fear for personal safety. Secure leaders, though, those who know that provision, protection, and promotion are theirs already, are able to make decisions based on principles and sound reasoning, with no thought for their own position. These are the leaders that people are crying out for, both in the Church and in the world.

Chapter 11

God, Through The Ages

For almost two thousand years, one of the foundational doctrines of Christianity has been that of the Trinity-that God is one God, but three persons.[1] The concept of the Trinity began developing from early in the first century, then was more succinctly defined by an early Church father named Tertullian, who first used the term "trinity." The refining of the doctrine continued on into the Council at Nicea, which stated in their creed that Jesus is "God of God, Light of Light, very God of very God, begotten, not made, being of one

---

1   Bible-Knowledge.com, "The Doctrine of the Trinity" http://www.bible-knowledge.com/trinity-god-jesus-holy-spirit.

substance with the Father."[2] With this creed, the doctrine of the Trinity was mostly settled, and never again became a serious issue of controversy. In later years, almost every denomination and movement has sought to define their particular interpretation of this essential doctrine, but almost all agree as to the basic tenets. Here is an example of such a statement from the Southern Baptist Convention:

"The eternal triune God reveals Himself to us as Father, Son, and Holy Spirit, with distinct personal attributes, but without division of nature, essence, or being."[3]

Throughout the Scripture, the progression of God's revelation of Himself is evident. The Old Testament is primarily the story of God the Father, though Christ is evident in "veiled" fashion (see Luke 24:27), and the Holy Spirit is given occasionally for fulfillment of a specific assignment, such as Bezalel creating art for the temple, or the Spirit of the Lord coming upon Gideon and other of Israel's judges. Essentially, though, the Old Testament is the story of God as Father, calling Adam his son (Luke 3:38) and referring to Israel collectively as "son" in Exodus

---

2   Religion Facts, "The Doctrine of the Trinity" http://www.religionfacts.com/christianity/beliefs/trinity.htm.

3   Ibid.

4:22: "Then you will say to Pharaoh: This is what the Lord says: Israel is My firstborn son."

This revelation of God as Father comes to fruition with the appearance of Jesus, who is called the "only begotten" Son of God (John 3:16), and is reiterated numerous times by Jesus Himself, and again when the writer to the Hebrews declares that *"Long ago God spoke to the fathers by the prophets at different times and in different ways. In these last days, He has spoken to us by [His] Son, whom He has appointed heir of all things and through whom He made the universe."* (Hebrews 1:1-2)

With the incarnation of Jesus, God the Son takes center stage in history. Any cursory examination of the New Testament Gospel writings proclaim the Sonship of Jesus, and simultaneously shout that God the Father is revealed in the Son. (John 1:18, John 14:7) Then, in what must have been a remarkable turn of events for those who walked with Him, Jesus suddenly announces that He is leaving, but that He will send someone to come alongside them, to literally live inside of them, who will speak to them and empower their lives. And so, on the day of Pentecost, God is revealed in the person of the Holy Spirit, and the fullness of God takes up residence in the heart of man. Consequently, we can follow the tracings of God's revelation of Himself to man in three distinct stages: first, Father, then the Son, and finally the Holy Spirit.

THE RE-REVELATION OF GOD

After the first century, Church history embarks on a long and winding road of definition and controversy that ultimately leads to the Dark Ages, where the light of the gospel was hidden by the mammoth forces of religion and political power for hundreds of years. Then, on October 31, 1517, when Martin Luther challenged the established religious power structure to debate ninety-nine points of contention, the door was opened for God to be revealed to the common man again.

On through the seventeenth, eighteenth and nineteenth centuries, salvation by grace alone became the battlecry of Christianity, and the Church began to operate once again as the "pillar and foundation of the truth." (1 Timothy 3:15) Awakenings swept entire countries, revivals reignited a long dormant fire of God in the hearts of multitudes, and preachers rose up in boldness and conviction, from the Wesley brothers and George Whitefield, to Charles Finney, Evan Roberts, and later to Billy Sunday and Billy Graham.

The twentieth century began with a different aspect of the revelation of God, one that had been little seen or spoken of since the early Church. Beginning in April of 1906 and continuing until about 1915, what became known as the Azusa Street Revival in large part re-introduced the person of the Holy Spirit into Church life as a source of transforming power and personal experience. This birthing of the Pentecostal movement gave rise to decades of Holy Spirit-infused theology and practice, and made household names of preachers like Smith Wigglesworth, Oral Roberts, and Kathryn Kuhlman.

The 1970s brought a fresh recognition of the Son of God as the only way to the Father through the Jesus Movement that originated with the hippie and rock culture of Southern California. What is now referred to as Contemporary Christian Music emerged from these previously disillusioned musicians and seekers who now had found that Jesus satisfied all of their longings. As the 1970s became the 1980s, the Jesus Movement mixed with Pentecostalism to bring about the Charismatic Renewal, which reached into virtually every denomination in America and saw people and churches ranging from Southern Baptist to Catholic embracing this new move of God. And now, as the first decade of the new century falls behind us, God, who has been re-revealing Himself in reverse order (first the Spirit, then the Son) seems to be speaking to the Body of Christ globally about the utmost importance and inescapably foundational household model of the Father and how He relates to His sons and daughters.

This is not to say that He hasn't already been speaking about issues of His Fatherhood. Especially as our society has witnessed the increasing breakdown of the role and influence of fathers, books and teachings on the Fatherhood of God have abounded. The problem, though, lay not with the theology of God as Father. Instead, it can be found in the fact that, even if we understand all about His goodness as a Father, we miss that goodness in our own lives if we see ourselves as orphans. This is the crux of the matter. We can proclaim that we are "King's kids" and we can begin all of our prayers with "Our Father," but if, in the depths of our hearts, we somehow believe that the great love of God is only available for those Christians more worthy than we are, we lose the great benefits of that great love. If we fail to see that we are fully-righted, fully-privileged children of the Living God, then we live our lives, not as true sons, but as urchins looking in the window, always hoping to be invited inside— into a house in which we already belong.

Chapter 12

For This Reason

Why did Jesus come? At first glance, it might seem an elementary question to ask, but it is in fact, multi-layered. There is any number of levels at which this question can be answered, such as:

> The Vacation Bible School level: "to die for my sins."
>
> The Sunday School level: "to die for *our* sins."
>
> The Average Christian level: "to get me to heaven."
>
> The Little-Bit-More-Mature Christian Level: "to give us abundant life."

While all of these are inherently right, there is a deeper aspect of truth to each of them. In fact, as we look at Scripture, we can see that the reasons given for Jesus' journey on the earth are multi-faceted. The more we walk around and look at the subject, the more the light of revelation glints off every surface of it. For instance, 1 John 3:8 tells us that "The Son of God appeared for this purpose, to destroy the works of the devil." (NAS) Luke 4:43 quotes Jesus as saying, "I must proclaim the good news about the kingdom of God to the other towns also, because I was sent for this purpose." Again, Jesus says about Himself in John 3:17, "For God did not send His Son into the world that He might condemn the world, but that the world might be saved through Him." And all three of those purposes swirl around the same center—Jesus came to rescue us.

There is another passage, though, where we get to listen in as Jesus converses with His Father right before He is arrested. And in this passage, we hear Jesus summing up, if you will, what He has seen as His purpose: "I have glorified You on the earth by completing the work You gave Me to do... I have revealed Your name to the men You gave Me from the world." (John 17:4,6) Obviously, Jesus means more than that He has simply told them God's name. The Greek word translated "name" here is the word *onoma*. It is used for "everything which the name covers, everything the thought or feeling of which is aroused in the mind by mentioning, hearing, remembering, the name, i.e. for one's rank, authority, interests, pleasure, command, excellences, deeds etc."[4] So essentially, Jesus is saying, "Father, mission accomplished. I have revealed who *You* are to the ones you gave me." Jesus considered His job well done in that He introduced His disciples to the Father.

And that is what made Jesus so different from anyone who came before Him. No one who had ever walked the earth had the power or authority to put on display the absolute fullness of who the Father is, the stark, unfiltered, undiluted person of God Himself. And He spent three and a half years doing just that.

"We've Never Heard That Before…"

"He was praying in a certain place, and when He finished, one of His disciples said to Him, 'Lord, teach us to pray, just as John also taught his disciples.' He said to them, 'Whenever you pray, say: Father…'" (Luke 11:1-2)

Now we don't know exactly what John taught His disciples, but it's a pretty safe guess that he didn't teach them what Jesus was teaching them. Remember, this request came immediately after

4   BibleStudyTools.com, New Testament Greek Lexicon, http://www.biblestudytools.com/lexicons/greek/nas/onoma.html.

Jesus had finished praying. Can't you just see the disciples sitting, listening, waiting. Not wanting to interrupt, yet anxious to do what He was doing. I believe that what made their ears perk up like a child who hears the ice cream truck, was something Jesus said in His prayers that they had never heard before: "Father…"

Remember also, that the disciples were no strangers to hearing people pray. They had grown up hearing the Pharisees pray, both in the synagogues and on the street corners, loud, long, repetitious prayers. But here was something different. Not once had they ever heard anyone speak to God as "Father." But somehow they knew that Jesus would make it possible for them to pray the same way— out of a relationship with God Himself, sons speaking with the Father.

In Matthew chapters 5 and 6, where this Model Prayer is taught first, it is in context of what is referred to as the Sermon on the Mount. In those two chapters, God is called Father 15 times. 10 of those are found in the phrase "your Father," and once, He is called "Our Father." Right out of the gate in His ministry, Jesus repeats this concept over and over, practically shouting what would be the bedrock truth of everything He would do and say for the next three years: it's all about a relationship. But not only that, it's all about a *family* relationship. As Pastor Andy Taylor of Sayre, Oklahoma has said, "If God had wanted something other than a family, He would have had us call Him something other than 'Father.'"

One of the greatest and most quoted of all Scriptures is found at the end of Matthew 6: "But seek first the kingdom of God and His righteousness, and all these things will be provided for you." (v.33) Its power, though, comes from the context in which it is set. No one starts a sentence with the word "but" without some confidence that the hearer knows what they have just said. And what Jesus has just said, was "So don't worry, saying, 'What will we eat?' or 'What will we drink?' or 'What will we wear?' For the idolaters eagerly seek all these things, and your *heavenly Father* knows that you need them." (Matt. 6:31-32; emphasis mine) In other words, the very thing that allows you the opportunity to seek the rule and reign of God in your life and in this world with full assurance that you don't have to worry about your own life, is sonship. It is predicated on your relationship with God as your Father and the comfort, joy, and freedom that relationship brings.

WHAT'S IN A NAME?

Up until the point when Jesus steps onto the scene, God had been referred to by many names, each of which exemplified an attribute of His character. The list includes names like:

- Provider
- My Banner
- Peace
- Lord of Hosts
- Sanctifier
- Our Righteousness
- God of Israel
- Healer
- Mighty One
- Holy One
- Judge
- The One Who Sees
- Everlasting God
- Strength
- Shield

Obviously, this list is not exhaustive, but it represents how God was revealing Himself to the world, especially through His people. It is of significant interest, though, that when Jesus chose a name to let us know to whom He would introduce us, He said this: "No one comes to the Father except through Me." (John 14:6b) And even in this verse, all of the other names of God are represented in this one. Look at the first half of this verse: "Jesus told him, 'I am the way, the truth, and the life.'" (John 14:6a) The reason this is so important is because when Israel was in the wilderness, they related to God through the ministry of the Tabernacle, especially the presence of God that would invade the innermost sanctum, the Most Holy Place, or the Holy of Holies, once a year on the Day of Atonement. On that day, the full impact of who God is would be manifested powerfully as He would take up residence in the small room where only the High Priest could enter. In that Tabernacle, there were three doorways. The first one, that led from the open land surrounding the tabernacle into the outer court, was called The Way. The next doorway, a veil that separated the outer court from the inner court, where the High Priest would prepare Himself to meet God, was called the Truth. And the third, the thick veil that separated the inner court from the Holy of Holies, was, as you might have guessed by now, called The Life. In that Most Holy Place, the God who was known by all of those names listed would, one day a year, step down in all of His manifest glory and overwhelming presence, and would meet the representative of man in order to cover their sins for another year.

And in that context, Jesus says, "If you come through Me, you, too, can know that very same God. But you will know Him, not just as Creator, or Judge, or Sanctifier, or even Peace or Healer. Because of Me, you will know Him as I do—as Father."

Chapter 13

Show Us The Father

And now, immediately after that world-shattering statement, Jesus continues:

" 'If you know Me, you will also know My Father. From now on you do know Him and have seen Him.' 'Lord,' said Philip, 'show us the Father, and that's enough for us.' Jesus said to him, 'Have I been among you all this time without your knowing Me, Philip? The one who has seen Me has seen the Father. How can you say, "Show us the Father"?' " (John 14:7-9)

It is good for us to point out here that Philip's statement was an absolutely true one: "Show us the Father, and that's enough for us." When we see God as Father, when we can know Him the way Jesus knows

Him, we will be well and truly satisfied. We find ourselves at home, confident and secure, comforted and belonging. If we only see God as Judge, we know that we have not measured up to the standard. If we know Him only as Sanctifier, we see how much further we have to go. Even if we only know Him as Provider, we aren't sure just how much provision we can expect, because surely it must be based on our performance.

But when we see the Father, we see ourselves as sons and daughters, adopted, privileged, co-heirs with Jesus. At least we should. It is very possible, as we have stated earlier, to know God is our Father, and still see ourselves as orphans. But Jesus' remedy for that was not to show us how wonderful we are, it was to continue to reveal the Father. Which, by the way, He did constantly, in many ways.

THE STORY OF THE LOST SON'S FATHER

Undoubtedly, one of the most trusted, well-known, and oft-preached parables of Jesus is the one commonly known as the Prodigal Son. However, because the word "prodigal" is not normally used in today's vernacular, newer translations of the Bible often call it the Story of the Lost Son, which is a little more accurate anyway. That's because it is the third part of a trilogy, following the parables of the

Lost Sheep and the Lost Coin. It might be even more accurate, though, to say that it is really the story of the Lost Son's Father. He, in fact, is the protagonist on which the tale turns. It is he who acts unpredictably, from the moment he actually gives his youngest son the inheritance.

But because the father is the pivotal character, his faithfulness and goodness stands in stark contrast to the behavior of both of his boys. Another name for this parable might be The Story of The Two Orphans. You see, both the lost son and his older brother had orphan hearts. The only difference was that one of them stayed home.

"He also said: "A man had two sons. The younger of them said to his father, 'Father, give me the share of the estate I have coming to me.' So he distributed the assets to them. Not many days later, the younger son gathered together all he had and traveled to a distant country, where he squandered his estate in foolish living." (Luke 15:11-13)

Obviously, the younger son was operating from the mindset of an orphan in one major aspect: he was utterly self-referential. Orphans think and live as if everything is ultimately about them. The very fact that the son was even asking for his inheritance up front was a way of saying, "Come on, old man, can't you die already? I'm anxious to get my life going but I can't do it without the money that is coming to me!" The incredibly brazen request demonstrated loudly that the young man was bereft of respect for his father, the one from whose loins he had sprung. And Jesus' listeners knew it, too. You can almost hear the gasps of shock and offense when Jesus quotes the son. No one in his right mind would speak to his father in such a way!

BETWEEN THE LINES

We need to pause for a moment to hear what else Jesus was clearly implying. In order to interpret Scripture correctly, we need to first ask the question, "What time is it?" In other words, where on the timeline of God's revelation of Himself and His plan for the world is this event taking place? The answer here is that Jesus is making His point at a moment when the Son of God has appeared to the nation of Israel, but they are actively rejecting Him as such. The three parables Jesus is teaching in Luke 15 are introduced this way: "All the tax collectors and sinners were approaching to listen to Him. And the Pharisees and scribes were complaining, "This man welcomes sinners and eats with them!" So He told them this parable…" (Luke 15:1-3)

This also answers the next interpretational question we must ask, which is "Who is the original audience? What did this parable mean to its intended hearers?" As we have seen, Jesus is speaking directly to the Pharisees here, with the tax collectors and sinners getting to listen in. So, knowing how the Pharisees felt about their own pious performance and reputation, who would Jesus be casting as the younger son? Not them, obviously, because they would never treat God in such a way. The only option then is everybody else— Jewish sinners and pagan Gentiles. And it fits. Paul writes in Romans chapter 1 about people who reject God's revelation of Himself, which as we have seen is primarily as Father. He characterizes them this way: "For though they knew God, they did not glorify Him as God or show gratitude. Instead, their thinking became nonsense, and their senseless minds were darkened… And because they did not think it worthwhile to have God in their knowledge, God delivered them over to a worthless mind to do what is morally wrong." (Romans 1:21, 28) And so the younger son, who should and could have known the father correctly, chooses to live for himself.

So, the younger son goes off to the big city, parties, spends all his money, loses all his party friends, and finds himself feeding pigs in a pigsty, which can only be described as below rock bottom for a Jewish boy. He then comes to his senses, figures that the servants in his father's house have it better than him, and decides to ask for a job there. Here we see another aspect of his orphan heart rising to the surface. He thinks that he has forfeited his relationship with the father and his status as a son through his mistakes. He relegates himself to position of servant and aspires to no more. So, he rehearses his speech and makes his way home.

The father, though, has never given up on his wayward son, and has held his position in the house and in the family secure for his inevitable return. One evening, he sees a puff of dust at the end of the long driveway, and he knows immediately who it is. The father runs to his son, hugs him, kisses him on the neck, and before his boy can even finish his speech, the father interrupts him, restores him to his rightful place, and as signified by the ring and robe, even restores his inheritance!

But wait a minute. Didn't he already spend his inheritance? Yep. But, as a son of the father, he never actually loses it. There is more where that came from. Even more shocking, the father doesn't say, "Well, I wish I could reinstate your inheritance, but let that be a lesson to you. There has to be some consequence to your actions, and that's it. Someday, even though you have returned and repented, you will still die penniless. Welcome home, son!"

No! Remember who is telling this story— Jesus! The storyteller is the One who is full of grace and truth, the One who is about to be torn and nailed to a cross so that all of the prodigals who will ever walk this earth can, through the forgiveness and boundless love of the Father, have their inheritance restored, even though they have spent a lifetime squandering it! In Jesus, no one dies an orphan!

ENTER ORPHAN #2, STAGE RIGHT

Now his older son was in the field; as he came near the house, he heard music and dancing. So he summoned one of the servants and asked what these things meant. 'Your brother is here,' he told him, 'and your father has slaughtered the fattened calf because he has him back safe and sound.' "Then he became angry and didn't want to go in. So his father came out and pleaded with him. But he replied to his father, 'Look, I have been slaving many years for you, and I have never disobeyed your orders, yet you never gave me a young goat so I could celebrate with my friends. But when this son of yours came, who has devoured your assets with prostitutes, you slaughtered the fattened calf for him.' " 'Son,' he said to him, 'you are always with me, and everything I have is yours. But we had to celebrate and rejoice, because this brother of yours was dead and is alive again; he was lost and is found.' " (Luke 15:26-32)

And now we see that the younger son was not the only one who thought like an orphan. Because, you see, rebellion is not the only sign of an orphan heart. The older son was just as self-referential as his little brother. To him, his sense of worth came from his work ethic and faithfulness to serve his father, not from his relationship with the father or position as a son. We see his orphan heart in his insecurity. "What about me? I never left, but I didn't get a party! He doesn't deserve your favor, I do!" And, of course, again we think about the Pharisees, who were to rightfully receive the brunt of this point. They assumed that, since they had kept the Law, God owed them something. They had not flaunted their sin like the tax collectors, prostitutes, and Gentiles. Surely this story can't be an accurate reflection of who God is!

And yet, as we have already seen, Jesus was constantly, intentionally revealing the heart and character of the Father in ways that had never been seen before. The good news for the older brother was that he didn't have to miss out on anything, either! If he could rise above his petty jealousies and judgments, he, too, could have a party with the Father whenever he wanted. The mind-blowing, paradigm-shattering statement to him was, "Everything I have is yours!" For both sons, the one factor that was to define their existence was not how good or bad they had been— it was to be the fact that they were blessed and favored for one reason: they were both sons of the father.

And so it is with us. None of us has ever earned our position with God, nor could we. The ground is level at the foot of the cross. Paul writes extensively in Romans chapters 1 through 3 to make the point that the whole world is equally guilty before God, but the good news of the gospel is that, because of the sacrifice of Jesus, that "to the one who does not work, but believes on Him who declares righteous the ungodly, his faith is credited for righteousness." (Romans 4:5). Is there any more glorious phrase in Scripture than "Him who declares righteous the ungodly"? If there is, it would have to be this one: "How happy the man whom the Lord will never charge with sin!" (Romans 4:8)

That is the blessing of the sons of God. We, the ungodly, are declared righteous because of Jesus' faithfulness, not our own. And, because of Him, the only begotten Son who died to become the firstborn of many brethren, we are those who can live in confidence and security, knowing that we will never be charged with sin! Never!

Let the party begin!

Chapter 14

Like Father, Like Son

When I was growing up, television still showed cigarette commercials. In the midst of those, though, there was one public service spot that was particularly memorable. It showed scenes of a loving father and his little boy, around five years old or so. As the dad painted the house on his tall ladder, his little boy slapped on a few brushstrokes from his smaller one. As the dad drove the convertible and stuck out his hand to indicate a turn, the little boy did the same with his toy steering wheel and a hand out his side of the car. When dad washed the car with the garden hose, the son squirted water on the wheels with a water gun and wiped it with a rag. Each scene ended with a voiceover that said, "Like father, like son," with playful music in the background. And when they took a walk and sat under a tree, the father took out a pack of cigarettes, lit one, and then carelessly laid the pack between himself and the boy. And, of course, the son picked up the cigarettes, looked into the pack, then looked at his father, while the voiceover said, "Like father, like son? Think about it."

Of course with our great level of sophistication today, that spot seems quaint and old fashioned, but it was so powerful that it ran from September 1967 until 1982. That's 15 years of "Like father, like son." Why did it resonate so powerfully? Because it made people stop smoking? Probably not, though it might have made some parents think twice before laying a pack of cigarettes within easy reach of a five-year-old. No, its power was in its root message: "What the father does, the son will do."

Jesus said something remarkably similar in John 5:19. While being attacked yet again by the Pharisees for healing on the Sabbath, He said: "I assure you: the Son is not able to do anything on His own, but only what He sees the Father doing. For whatever the Father does, the Son also does these things in the same way." In that one incredible statement, Jesus essentially whisked us out of the audience and brought us behind the scenes of His entire earthly ministry. People had been following Him by the droves for years, watching Him do miraculous and wondrous works.

But suddenly, Jesus does here what no good magician does- He revealed His secret. That's because He wasn't a magician, He was a Son! Jesus never intended to wow the crowds with great feats of prestidigitation, He was trying to model for us what would soon be available to us through the Holy Spirit. He was showing us what sons and daughters do! They live out of intimate relationship with God Himself.

This is the antidote to Christian Celebrity Syndrome. In our orphan hearts, not knowing or believing that we can have the same power of God that we see in our spiritual heroes, we follow them around like a suckerfish on a shark. The revelation of your identity as a son or daughter of God is the answer. When you see that your value is in who you are, not what you do, you will find that you no longer have the need to impress anyone. When the only person whose smile matters is the Father, you will find that there is really only one star on the stage– Jesus, the Only Begotten Son.

"Exorcisms R Us"

If you haven't read this story from Acts chapter 19 recently, here it is again, to perfectly illustrate our point:

"God was performing extraordinary miracles by Paul's hands, so that even facecloths or work aprons that had touched his skin were brought to the sick, and the diseases left them, and the evil spirits came out of them. Then some of the itinerant Jewish exorcists attempted to pronounce the name of the Lord Jesus over those who had evil spirits, saying, "I command you by the Jesus whom Paul preaches!" Seven sons of Sceva, a Jewish chief priest, were doing this. The evil spirit answered them, "Jesus I know, and Paul I recognize-but who are you?" Then the man who had the evil spirit leaped on them, overpowered them all, and prevailed against them, so that they ran out of that house naked and wounded." (Acts 19:11-16)

That probably shouldn't be one of my favorite stories in the whole Bible, but it is. This is our first recorded example of Celebrity Christianity Syndrome. These sons of a Jewish chief priest had obviously been convinced that what was happening through Paul was genuine. They had been following him around, taking notes, and measuring results. So, they did the next logical thing— they started their own exorcism business. The problem, though, is that they were only sons of Sceva, not sons of God. You see, this is what the orphan heart does. It watches what happens when a son of God relates intimately with the Father, bringing Heaven to earth. But all the orphan sees is cause and effect. Say this, get that. When in reality, a lot more had already been happening behind the scenes. As evidenced by the rest of Scripture, Paul was constantly praying, listening to the Holy Spirit, getting direction on what to do next. He never took for granted that he ever had a formula that would work without constant communication with the Father.

But Seven Sons, Inc. didn't see that part. They just saw the results and figured that they knew how to get them. And it didn't work. No surprise to us, really, but I imagine the epic failure of their business model came as quite a shock to them. And, even as we chuckle to ourselves, shake our heads, and tsk tsk their naivete, don't we do the same thing? Did you happen to see verse 12 above? It's the one that says that facecloths and work aprons that had touched Paul's skin were laid on the sick and they were healed. Have you ever just assumed that to be a formula for healing just because it shows up in the Bible? Don't get me wrong, I'm not saying God might not use that same method today. But it has to flow out of your intimate, hearing connection with the Father such that you know it is what He has said directly to you, for a specific time and a particular reason. You see, orphans see the results that sons get, then they try to formulate it so that it will work for them without going through all the steps of sonship— intimacy with God and hearing Him for themselves.

Let me show you how I recognized my orphan heart the same way.

No Shortcuts

When I was a young man, I was greatly impacted by a number of great preachers, not the least of whom was the fiery Scottish preacher, Leonard Ravenhill. If you have ever read even a handful of pages in one of his books, or listened to just one of his messages, you know that Ravenhill pulled no punches. He could turn a phrase or level a gaze, and you knew that God was watching you. And, if you were even just a little bit open, the Holy Spirit would put his finger on your most sensitive hidden area and bring it into the light. The fact was, after hearing Leonard Ravenhill preach, you either marched away mad, or you ran to the altar in tears.

And so, as my friends and I began preaching, we knew we could do worse than to model our preaching after Ravenhill. The problem was, we weren't him. I doubt any of us spent a fraction of the time with God that Ravenhill did every day, and it never dawned on us that he had at least 50 years of wisdom, maturity, experience and unction on us, all put together. Still, that didn't stop us. We would go wherever we could— retreats, youth camps, country churches, downtown street corners— and deliver the fire. And to us, in our boldness, and even though we really loved Jesus and wanted people to know him, our measuring stick— mine, at least— was all wrong. I remember feeling that people could either get mad or get right, it didn't matter which. And if someone didn't tell me after the sermon that it really stepped on their toes, I hadn't done my job. Worse yet, just let someone tell me that they actually enjoyed it! What?!? Were they not even listening?

I acted as if the secret to Leonard Ravenhill's "success" was his cleverness, his delivery, his willingness to offend the hearer. And way too often, I succeeded in all of those areas. That was my orphan heart. Now, though, I see that the great power in Ravenhill's message did not reside in the pulpit or the page. It came from the prayer closet. It was birthed in tears and travail. Ravenhill paid the price to say what he said. I was wanting to have the same things he had in ministry, but I was trying to get it on credit and pay later.

Years later, after I had mellowed and matured a bit, I found myself pastoring a small Baptist church in Flower Mound, Texas. After about a year of pastoring there, much to my sincere amazement, we had not grown from 100 to 4,000 as I had expected. So, obviously, I had to find the secret to church growth. Lucky for me, not everyone was toiling in obscurity like I was, so there were plenty of church growth models to be had. At that time, two of the fastest growing churches in the country were Saddleback Church and Willow Creek Community Church under the leadership of Rick Warren and Bill Hybels, respectively. I had heard Rick Warren speak at a conference in Fort Worth a few years earlier, and was aware of the impact that Willow Creek was having in the Chicago area. So, I picked one. I obtained a video of Bill Hybels preaching a wonderful evangelistic message, and studied it. I memorized his points, his style, his jokes. I made replicas of his visual aids. Then, I scheduled a special evangelistic service on a Saturday night (the only cool time to have a church service in those days), and encouraged the people in my little church to invite all of their lost friends for an evening that would change their eternity!

The big night came, and I made sure to dress for success. I wore business casual pants, a blazer, and a shirt buttoned all the way up with a bolo tie. Very cool. I prepared, I prayed, and I waited for the throng. I opened the doors, and in they came! My wife, three of my church members, and one unchurched man brought by one of them. But I held nothing back. Clever illustrations, impressive props, and an impassioned plea filled the next 45 minutes. And at the end, the one lost man in the audience was absolutely, completely, unmistakably… underwhelmed. I believe now that it was because even though my intentions were pure, I was trying to fight a battle in someone else's armor. I was focusing on trying to formulate Warren's and Hybels' success, but what I missed was that they got their visions for ministry and for their cities directly from the throne, not from the copy machine.

When Paul said in 1 Corinthians 4:13, "Therefore, I urge you, be imitators of me," he was not saying "Dress like me, copy my mannerisms and idiosyncracies, and use my jokes." He was actually appealing to them as *sons*! Here is the same verse in context: *"I'm not writing this to shame you, but to warn you as my dear children. For you can have 10,000 instructors in Christ, but you can't have many fathers. Now I have fathered you in Christ Jesus through the gospel. Therefore I urge you, be imitators of me. This is why I have sent to you Timothy, who is my beloved and faithful child in the Lord. He will remind you about my ways in Christ Jesus, just as I teach everywhere in every church."* (1 Corinthians 4:14-17) Like father, like son. Even though Paul was unashamed to hold up his own life as an example, he was still pointing his spiritual sons in the house to the only Begotten Son, the One who said He and the Father are one: "[Timothy] will remind you about my ways in Christ Jesus…"

"Watch me," Paul is saying. "Watch me listen to the Father. Watch me as I magnify Jesus. Watch me follow the Holy Spirit. If I succeed, watch me point people to Jesus. And if I fall, watch me get up." And Paul said all of these things, not because these are the things that teachers say. These are the things that a father says.

THE THREE KEYS TO THE SEVEN WAYS TO THE FIVE SECRETS OF WHATEVER

It is good and right for us to seek new ways of breaking down complicated information and ideas into understandable, accessible bites that people can easily digest. There is a difference, though, between doing that and looking for the secret formula. I am wary of anything that offers me the "three simple steps" to whatever I am looking for if it has anything at all to do with my relationship with God. Those kinds of books and conferences appeal only to the orphan in me, looking for an easy way to the results I think I need to feel valuable in the Kingdom. It's like the spiritual version of yo-yo dieting. Millions of people have lost and gained the same 10 or 20 pounds year after year, because the idea of a quick fix is intoxicating. "I heard this minister pray this over a woman when she was healed, so that must be the phrase that gets God to move. Finally! I have discovered the secret of power with God!" And so we pray for someone in the same condition, and it seems nothing happens. And little do we realize that the minister we heard pray, has never prayed that for anyone before or since. It came from his communion with God and a well-honed, practiced ability to hear the Holy Spirit in that moment.

A couple of years ago, I was dangerously close to burnout. Some good friends of mine saw it and knew how to rescue me. Working with my church, they sent me on an eight-week sabbatical, to do nothing but get empty and rest— which, it turns out, is hard work at first.

At the end of week 2, I started a Sabbatical Journal. The Lord spoke something to me about what I was going through, then He was strangely silent until the end of the whole eight weeks. Here is my journal entry from that second week:

Monday, June 28, 2010

2:28 am

Ever since my first sermon at Loachapoka Baptist Church, and probably even before, I have been wearing someone else's suit. For the past 31 years, I have performed, both as a preacher and a pastor, in like manner of the best men that I had watched in that position. This has not necessarily been a bad thing, mind you, but still, I have modeled my pastoral style after those who have come before me. The problem, though, is that it has become Saul's armor for me. I have tailored my motivations, my goals, my preaching style, my counseling style, everything I do, to an idea in my head of what those great and godly men have done. But, in the final analysis, it isn't me. Somewhere inside all that armor is a David trying to get out.

So what is "me"? I have no idea. That is what I am going to spend the next six weeks trying to get to. My friend told me that this was going to be like peeling an onion, and he was right. I don't know how many layers I will have to strip away to find who I really am, but that is what I will do. Right now, I don't even know how to go about doing it, but I am confident that the Lord will reveal it. What's more, I don't really have a clue as to what I will find at the center of me, but whatever it is, that's who I will be. And that is what I will pastor from, preach from, be relational from, for the rest of my life.

I sure hope this works.

It did work. Not because I took eight weeks off. But because in that eight weeks, I rediscovered my identity as a son of the Only Living God.

I urge you, beloved sons and daughters of God— joint heirs with Christ and ambassadors of a greater Kingdom— shed Saul's armor. Stop looking for the magic formula. Just take your place as a son or daughter in the Father's house. Then take a deep breath of the atmosphere of grace, believe that everything that belongs to the Father really is yours because of Jesus, then just walk into the living room, sit down on the couch, and stay there until you know who you really are.

Chapter 15

Free People, Free People

So what difference does confident sonship make in the world? As Apostle Paul is deep in discussion of the nature of sonship in Romans 8, he says in verse 14 that "the creation eagerly waits with anticipation for God's sons to be revealed." But what do they look like when they are revealed? How will the watching world recognize us? What kind of impact do sons make on their world? First, let's look a little more closely at how Jesus defines the life of sonship in Matthew chapter 11.

In Matthew 11:23, Jesus says: "Come to Me, all of you who are weary and burdened, and I will give you rest." One of the interpretations that I have heard over the years goes something like this: "Life can get tough, and you are going to have to work really hard, but if you accept me as your Savior, then one day, when you die, you will get to rest." Now, I'm not going to argue that that is entirely without value, but I do think that it entirely misses the point of what Jesus was saying. For some, the above statement is the only good news they have ever found in the gospel, but let me suggest to you that the good news of the gospel in that verse is even better than the promise of an eternal weekend.

The key to this verse is found in the next two verses, 29-30: "All of you, take up My yoke and learn from Me, because I am gentle and humble in heart, and you will find rest for yourselves. For My yoke is easy and My burden is light." So here is another place where I think we have traditionally missed the point of the passage. I just assumed that the "yoke" in question referred to the wooden bow-shaped plow attachment that fit over the neck of a pair of oxen so that they could pull the plow. So, the verse naturally meant, "If you give your life to Me, you are still going to have to work hard, but somehow you will like it better." Again, still not what I would call the glorious good news of the gospel.

Free And Easy

I believe now that what Jesus was referring to was the same thing that He went on to talk about more specifically in Matthew 23:1-4: "Then Jesus spoke to the crowds and to His disciples: "The scribes and the Pharisees are seated in the chair of Moses. Therefore do whatever they tell you and observe [it]. But don't do what they do, because they don't practice what they teach. They tie up heavy loads that are hard to carry and put them on people's shoulders, but they themselves aren't willing to lift a finger to move them." You see, every Rabbi had a "yoke." The yoke was what the Jewish people called any particular Rabbi's specific interpretation of the Torah, or the Law. Each Rabbi would have a special slant, if you will, or a different take on how he interpreted the Law. Jesus says, though, that the "yoke" of the scribes and Pharisees was too much for the people to bear, and they didn't even try to help them carry it. The people were being crushed under the weight of the Law. They couldn't bear up under the requirements of righteousness necessary to please the heart of God and appease his judgment against sin. And the Pharisees kept their distance and shook their heads.

But Jesus has a better invitation: "Come to me. Take my yoke on you. My yoke is light and will not be a burden." (author's paraphrase) What was Jesus' yoke? What was His primary interpretation of the purpose and role of the Law? It is revealed in the verse leading up to his invitation, in Matthew 11:27: "All things have been entrusted to Me by My Father. No one knows the Son except the Father, and no one knows the Father except the Son and anyone to whom the Son desires to reveal Him." Jesus' yoke- His emphasis, His focus- was an invitation to know the Father like He knew the Father. And where the Pharisees wouldn't lift a finger to bear the heavy burden of the Law, Jesus would actually bear the full weight of the Law on Himself- He who knew no sin became sin for us- and take it off of our shoulders, putting it on his own in the shape of a cross. All so that we could know what it is to be sons and daughters of God, brought into the family on the shoulders of the only begotten Son.

And so His yoke is easy. That doesn't mean that life is always easy, because the yoke isn't "life." It is the life-giving, burden-lifting, freedom-bringing, prison-door-opening truth that we are now, at His invitation, sons and daughters of the living God, through no effort of our own, but resting fully on the gift of grace. So, we have been truly set free, not by our own faithfulness, but by the faithfulness of Jesus. And the life we are set free to live is one marked by what I will call Resurrectional Transformation.

You Think *That* Was Something!

In Matthew chapter 4, immediately after Jesus' temptation in the wilderness and the calling of His first disciples, we read the following words in verses

23-25: "Jesus was going all over Galilee, teaching in their synagogues, preaching the good news of the kingdom, and healing every disease and sickness among the people. Then the news about Him spread throughout Syria. So they brought to Him all those who were afflicted, those suffering from various diseases and intense pains, the demon-possessed, the epileptics, and the paralytics. And He healed them. Large crowds followed Him from Galilee, Decapolis, Jerusalem, Judea, and beyond the Jordan."

The very next verse begins chapter 5: "When He saw the crowds, he went up on the mountain, and after He sat down, His disciples came to him. Then he began to teach them..." (Matt. 5:1) And thus begins the Sermon on the Mount. So think with me for just a moment about who is hearing this sermon. It is the multitude of people who have been hearing the good news about the kingdom and then have seen the power of that kingdom demonstrated in their very lives. So basically, Jesus' method of teaching resembles the advice given to public speakers today: "Tell 'em what you're gonna tell 'em, tell 'em, then tell 'em what you just told 'em." Jesus, though, did more than just tell. He proclaimed the right-here-right-now-ness of the kingdom, showed them the power of that kingdom, and then, in the sermon on the mount, he told them more about what they had just seen. And in this context of people whose lives are being radically altered by the anointing of this Anointed One, as they are immersed in this atmosphere of Heaven and getting a glimpse into the not too distant future that Jesus would be creating for them on the cross, Jesus boldly and without hesitation paints a picture for them of the up-til-now unimaginable life that awaits them. In this sermon, he gives them five mind-blowing, life-shaking examples of the kind of transformation that this kingdom brings. They have already been impacted by the healing, delivering, revelatory power of the kingdom, but Jesus says, "Wait! There's more!"

He then proceeds to give them five illustrations of this new kingdom life that begin with "You have heard it said," and end with "But I tell you…" And the last of the five in Matthew 5 represents one of the most unthinkable, incomprehensible, brain-scrambling statements that any of them have ever heard: "You have heard that it was said, Love your friends and hate your enemies. But I tell you, love your enemies and pray for those who persecute you…" (Matt. 5:43) Jesus might as well have said, "Okay everybody, as you can see, the kingdom of God is here, so I want all of you to make yourselves grow three feet taller by this time next week." That would have been no less shocking for them to hear. The difference, though, is that He wasn't telling them to do something impossible. He was telling them that *He* was going to do something impossible *in* them. Jesus didn't die to set us free from a law that we couldn't keep, just to give us another law that we couldn't keep. Again, unlike the Pharisees, who tied heavy loads on the people that they couldn't carry, and wouldn't lift a finger to help them, Jesus would take our entire burden of the requirements of the law on His own shoulders, and carry it to the cross. So if he wasn't giving them a commandment that they couldn't obey, how were they ever supposed to live that kind of love? Jesus knew. They *would* be able to live it, and even *want* to live it, by way of a new heart, put into them through a new covenant, having been *transformed* by the resurrection life of Jesus in the person and presence of the soon-arriving Holy Spirit. Jesus wasn't giving them unachievable good advice, He was announcing the good news of what was about to be a reality for them.

One of my favorite preachers from many years ago was Roy Hession, who used to say, "I have heard many sermons in my life. Most of them have been good advice. Not many have been good news." The gospel is good news, not just good advice. It is the unbreakable promise from the very heart of God that "since by the one man's trespass, death reigned through that one man, how much more will those who receive the overflow of grace and the gift of righteousness reign in life through the one man, Jesus

Christ." (Romans 5:17) It is the irrefutable, rooftop-worthy news that we, "being buried with Him by baptism into death, in order that, just as Christ was raised from the dead by the glory of the Father, so we too may walk in a new way of life. For if we have been joined with Him in the likeness of His death, we will certainly also be in the likeness of His resurrection." (Romans 6:4-5)

Resurrectional transformation is not only possible for those who have received the kingdom, it is to be confidently expected. The good news that the kingdom has come, forgiveness is final, and there is now on the earth a new kind of people, brings a hope, an excitement-- an enthusiastic anticipation of a supernatural re-formation of the sin-marred devastation, into a Heaven-branded new creation. The gospel is not wishful thinking. The gospel is not "your life can be a little better if you are strong enough to make some changes." It is the unequivocal truth that what is wrong in you is made right in Jesus. What was lost has been found. What was orphaned is now a son. What was dead is suddenly alive.

This kind of resurrectional transformation can and should be expected to manifest wherever resurrection is needed. I wrote in a previous book, *The New Normal: Experiencing the Unstoppable Move of God*, about my friend Lee McDougald, who was dying of Parkinson's Disease. I had walked alongside him as he shuffled through three airports, but then, one night, as I stood beside him, I watched him be dramatically, absolutely, completely, utterly healed of "incurable" Parkinson's. That is transformation.

I also remember being overcome by the reality of the transforming power and presence of the rule and reign of God as I watched another friend, Delia Knox, pop out of her wheelchair and begin to walk for the first time in over 22 years. What began as an unsteady, unbalanced shuffle, before the end of the night became a high-stepping march, full of confidence and direction, and now she dances as she worships her Healer. That is transformation.

Recently, I met Charles (not his real name) from New York. When Charles was a boy of seven, a neighbor's big brother in his apartment complex took him under a stairwell and began to molest him for what would continue for two years. As Charles grew, he decided that he would never be touched, nor would he touch anyone, ever again. At the age of 60, Charles was a recluse. He weighed 365 pounds, cut his own shoulder-length hair to avoid going to a barber, and put cardboard over all of the windows in his apartment to keep out the light. One day, the wife of a local pastor who knew of Charles, took a friend to visit him. Out of sheer courtesy, he let them in and agreed to pray a prayer of salvation with them, but, as he says, even though he was just being polite, something happened.

The Holy Spirit began to speak to him. The Lord gave him a new way of eating and a desire to follow through, where numerous diets had failed him. Before long, he began to write worship songs, though he had never been musical in his life. He then found he had a real desire to be with fellow believers, so he sought out the pastor whose wife had prayed with him. Soon, he began to call the church office and sing these new songs over the answering machine, and the worship team learned the songs and incorporated them into their Sunday services. Just three years later, Charles has lost 115 pounds, he has written about 15 worship songs that his church regularly sings, and he waves the banners as he worships at the front of the church. When I met him at a retreat in North Carolina, he had never been off of Long Island. That week, he stayed in a hotel room for the first time. He packed a suitcase for the first time. He spent five days with about fifteen other men that he did not know. The first day, he was a bit withdrawn, but by the end of the week, he was leading us all in worship and he didn't want to leave. That is transformation.

I have an older sister named Debi, whom I barely knew growing up. From the age of thirteen, Debi was in and out of mental hospitals and bad relationships. One of my earliest memories of her is waking up to sound of her screaming because she had overdosed on some kind of pills, and then had decided that she didn't want to die. I was 7 years old when I looked out the window and saw my Dad running across the lawn with Debi in his arms, rushing her to the hospital. She went on to attempt suicide numerous times in the coming few years. Two weeks ago, I walked into our worship center at Deeper Life just before the start of our second morning service, and I saw my oldest sister, Debi, praying with the wife of one of my Elders. Four days later, on Thursday, Debi called me and said, "I just had to tell you something. Ever since I was thirteen years old, I have battled with bi-polar, racing thoughts that never let up, and fear of the night and the dark. But this morning, the Lord woke me up early and reminded me that ever since Sunday morning, my mind has been at rest, and I have had no fear of the dark or the night. Last Sunday, when we were singing that He 'breaks every chain,' He broke my chains. For the first time in 45 years, I am truly free." That is transformation.

And then there is Sam Noerr, or Andrew Turner, or Jorge Cancel, all of whom will tell you that after losing their long-held, good-paying jobs, they walked through months, in two cases over a year, with a new, confident assurance that as sons of the living God, that they need not be anxious, because the Father would faithfully provide for them and their wives and children. If they were writing this, they would tell you story after story, not only of how God has consistently cared for them, but how their own orphan hearts have found their identity as sons in the Father's house. Anxiety is now unnatural for them. That is transformation.

I believe it is significant that when Jesus was painting that radical picture of a transformed life of loving our enemies in Matthew 5, he followed it by saying to love that way "so you may be sons of your Father in Heaven." (Matt. 5:45) That phrase "so that you may be" is most accurately translated "so that you may *show yourselves to be* sons of your Father in Heaven." What does that mean? How does loving your enemies and praying for those who persecute you show that you are a son or daughter of God? Because when someone is secure as a son or daughter of God, they know that no enemy can hold sway over them. They know that nothing that anyone can do can separate them from the love of God that is in Christ Jesus. They know that if God is for them, who can be against them? And they are actually able to live that transformed life of wanting to pray for their enemies, hoping that their enemy will come to know the Father like they know the Father. That is transformation.

OLD NORMAL NO MORE

Jesus goes on to illustrate this truth of resurrectional transformation with the same kind of "compare and contrast" method that you hated to see appear on your English test in school. In Matthew 5:46-47, Jesus continues: "For if you love those who love you, what reward will you have? Don't even the tax collectors do the same? And if you greet only your brothers, what are you doing out of the ordinary? Don't even the Gentiles do the same?" In other words, if all you are capable of doing is being nice to those who are nice to you, being good to those who are good to you, what's the big deal about that? Anyone can do that! Don't expect God to reward you for doing what people without His presence can do. That is way too low a level of living to be normal for someone in whom the very Spirit of the resurrected Son of God has taken up residence! How can anyone see that you are a son or daughter of God if you can't do something that they can't do? Love is not only the law of the new covenant and the currency of Heaven, it is the identifying mark of those who are born of God. People who do not yet know Jesus can't love their enemies. Only those who have been transformed by the resurrection can do that.

FREE PEOPLE, FREE PEOPLE

In Luke 4:18, when Jesus stands to read in the synagogue, he reads from Isaiah 61 and announces that He is the Anointed One who will set the prisoner free, heal the broken-hearted, and lift up the downtrodden. That passage in Isaiah goes on to say that those people, the ones who have been so drastically transformed by the Anointed One, go on to fulfill a destiny themselves: "They will rebuild the ancient ruins; they will restore the former devastations; they will renew the ruined cities, the devastations of many generations."

You may have heard it said that "hurt people, hurt people." In other words, people who have been wounded, inevitably cause wounds in others. It may be true that hurt people hurt people, but it is also true that "free people, free people." Transformed people become agents of transformation. Forgiven people forgive people. They rebuild the ruins. They renew what was devastated by previous generations. They bring life where there once was death. They give out the anointing of the Anointed One who lives in them.

For such is the transforming power of the resurrection, in those who have been made alive again. Such is the power of a son.

Chapter 16

Have A Seat

The process of going from "orphan" to "son" is called adoption. The Apostle Paul uses this image very strategically when trying to help his readers understand what happened to them when they were brought into God's family. In Romans chapter 8, Paul uses the concept of adoption knowing that the Greco-Roman idea of adoption, which the church in Rome understands, is very different from the Jewish concept, in which the New Covenant is based.

In the Greco-Roman culture, adoptions almost never came about as a result of compassion for children. The primary force driving Roman adoptions was the acquisition of an heir where there was none. In fact, it was often a requirement that the family be lacking an heir to even be approved for an adoption. However, there was a very strong aspect to the Roman adoption model that Paul wanted the Romans to get if they were to understand who they were in Christ: "One of the strengths of Roman adoption was its complete acceptance of the adoptee. Once a child had been adopted, everything from their past was erased. While they still had a blood connection with their former parents, the legal and familial ties to them were entirely severed. An adoptee in Roman society was endowed with all of the rights, privileges, and responsibilities of his new family just as though he was a natural born son. The adoptee was expected to respect and honor his new parents just as though they were his real parents."[5]

This fullness of inheritance is extremely important to Paul as he explains adoption. However, there was a drawback to how the Gentiles in the Roman church understood adoption, too: "The greatest drawback was the fact that at any time the adoptee could be emancipated by his adopted father. Emancipation revoked all the rights that one possessed by having been a part of the family. All property and inheritance rights were completely lost."[6]

---

5   Baina David King, Adoption in New Testament Times, Liberty University Senior Honors Papers, http://digitalcommons.liberty.edu/honors/186/ p 22.

6   Ibid.

And so, Paul weaves together both the Jewish and Roman practices of adoption when he puts those fears of rejection to rest in Romans 8:15-17: "For you did not receive a spirit that makes you a slave again to fear, but you received the Spirit of sonship. And by him we cry, ""Abba," Father." The Spirit himself testifies with our spirit that we are God's children. Now if we are children, then we are heirs--heirs of God and co-heirs with Christ, if indeed we share in his sufferings in order that we may also share in his glory."

When we were ministering together recently, my friend Kenny Thacker told a story that illustrates this truth perfectly. It concerns a couple that he knows, and their discovery of what sonship looks like. I'll change their names here for privacy, but the story is true.

A few years ago, Scott and Jennifer knew that it was time for them to adopt. They had a good life and a loving marriage, and they wanted to bring children into the blessing of their home. Scott and Jennifer were pretty well off, as we say in the South. They weren't the richest of the rich, but they had more than enough to be very comfortable. Sensing the leading of the Lord in adoption, they began the process of adopting two children, not yet teenagers, from an orphanage in Eastern Europe.

Finally, after all of the arrangements and approval, Scott and Jennifer flew to Eastern Europe to meet and bring home their new children. They met the boy and girl that would take their name, and fell deeply in love. These children, then, left the orphanage where they had lived for years, went with Scott and Jennifer, and boarded a plane for the first time in their lives. They flew over the ocean for the first time in their lives, and when they arrived in the United States, they climbed into what was the nicest vehicle they had ever seen in their lives.

This new family made their way from the airport and through the countryside, past the most beautiful cities and buildings that the children had ever seen. Soon, they pulled up in front of a house that was bigger than the one that belonged to the president of their country. When they entered the home, they were introduced to their new rooms. Each child had a bedroom that was tailored for them. Scott and Jennifer had researched these two young ones and had decorated each room with that child's favorite colors and motifs. The closets and drawers were full of brand new clothes, exactly in their size, and the beds were more grand than anything they had ever slept in before.

Scott and Jennifer showed them the kitchen, where the refrigerator and the pantry were stocked full of everything that they could want or need. Plenty of food of every kind was there for them, foods that they already loved, and foods that they had yet to discover. These two precious children, this new son and daughter, would lack for nothing.

Sometimes, though, when Scott or Jennifer would walk into their children's rooms to wake them in the morning, they would find them sleeping on the floor next to the bed. Other times, Jennifer would go to put folded clothes in their dressers and find food stuffed down deep in the drawers, hidden by socks and t-shirts. They had lived in an orphanage for too long. All they had known was that they had better get all of the food they could, when they could, because they never knew when it would be gone, or when someone might take it. Clothes had to be carefully guarded and hidden, so that they would still be there the next day. And the beds, obviously the beds just couldn't be for them to sleep on. They were too big and soft and nice, something that they could never be good enough to deserve.

It took months for these two children to learn how to be a son and a daughter of the house. Months to undo the patterns of lack and self-protection that they had learned in the hard world of the orphanage. Months to learn that they were, in fact, somewhere they had never been before— they were home.

As the truth of our adoption into the family of God truly begins to sink in, it may take us a while to learn how to be sons and daughters in His house. It may seem too good to be true that you really have a Father who freely gives you His presence, His pleasure, protection, provision, and promotion. But it is true. And when you finally realize that you don't have to sleep in the barn anymore like Brandon, that you don't have to hoard love and money and ambition and acceptance, and when you finally take that first step back into the house where all of the blessings of sonship are yours— when you step into that living room, the best thing you can do is just take a seat on the couch, look around, soak it all in, and just stay there until you really know who you are. No need to start performing, as if that's what got you into the house to begin with. And when you realize just how good you really have it as a son or daughter of God, you will gladly start to find your place in His family. Then, when you serve your Father, you will find that you are no longer trying to gain His favor or His acceptance. Finally, you will know what it is like to live *from* His blessing, not *for* it.

And then— finally— you will truly be free.

About the Title...

It seemed in order for me to let you know that I know what "hogwash" is.

Dictionary.com has this definition:

1. the refuse given to hogs; swill.
2. any worthless stuff.
3. meaningless or insincere talk, writing, etc.; nonsense; bunk.

I do hope, now that you have read the book, that you have recognized the play on words. You see, to the unbelieving world, the gospel presented in this little book is just that, it's hogwash—worthless stuff, meaningless talk, nonsense. But one of the great, unfathomable attributes of God is that He delights in taking something that seems like nonsense to the world, and He makes it the most profound, most beautiful, wisest and most breathtaking reality that the human heart has ever known. The truth of the gospel is that while the world thinks a pig cannot really be changed into anything beyond an ordinary, muddy, slop-eating little farm animal—well, the truth is, that God washes hogs and makes them sons. I continue to be absolutely awestruck by the middle of Romans 4:5, which speaks of God as "…Him who declares righteous the ungodly…" Even right smack dab in the middle of their ungodliness, when they "believe on Him," without even having done one righteous thing… He declares them righteous. God washes hogs. How do I know? Because I was once a hog. But now I'm a son. I was stained by sin. Now I'm clean. I was an orphan. But because of Jesus, now I'm an heir. I was ungodly. Now, by faith in Him, I am righteous.

And this is the beauty of the title of this tale. What the world thinks is un-doable, God has already done. And I hope that you, with me, can say that you are now a hog washed.

"Brothers, consider your calling: not many are wise from a human perspective, not many powerful, not many of noble birth. Instead, God has chosen the world's foolish things to shame the wise, and God has chosen the world's weak things to shame the strong.

God has chosen the world's insignificant and despised things-the things viewed as nothing-so He might bring to nothing the things that are viewed as something, so that no one can boast in His presence. But from Him you are in Christ Jesus, who for us became wisdom from God, as well as righteousness, sanctification, and redemption, in order that, as it is written: The one who boasts must boast in the Lord."

1 Corinthians 1:26-31

Recommended Reading

Frost, Jack. *Spiritual Slavery to Spiritual Sonship.* Shippensburg, PA: Destiny Image, 2006.

Gottfried, Mike, and Ron Benson. *Coach's Challenge: Faith, Football, and Filling the Father Gap.* New York: Howard, 2007.

Hall, Dudley. *Orphans No More: Learning to Live Loved.* Euless, TX: Kerygma Ventures Press, 2011.